TURKEY

WITHOUT THE TRIMMINGS

WORKING A
HOLIDAY RESORT – MY STORY

PAUL SLANEY

First published in paperback by
Michael Terence Publishing in 2024
www.mtp.agency

ISBN 9781800947320

Michael Terence
Publishing

Confessions, Advice & Thanks

I was just a normal kid brought up on a council estate and although I was never top of the class at Sir Leo Schultz comprehensive, I could always tell a good story. So, when I released my files to publishers they must have been horrified at the grammar and the way I rambled.
"You need a proofreader to make it perfect" I was told by many a prospective author.

Of course, I wanted my book to be perfect and knowing proofreaders don't come cheap, I had the money put aside to ensure it. So, off to the proofreader it went and it did indeed come back perfect... too perfect! I couldn't live with that! I don't profess to be Dickens, Shakespeare or Steven King, I didn't want it that perfect! After all, my time in Turkey was far from perfect. I wanted my readers to actually relive the reality of that time through my words.

When I began this book, I was simply a fella who had a story and slapped away at my keyboard reliving my story as if it was yesterday. The memories were vivid because, quite frankly, they were the best of my life.
My target audience is predominantly the British holidaymakers that holiday in Turkey. The majority of which are like me, just normal people with a working-class background who don't particularly want to judge my book on how it's been written but by its content.
My book is written how I lived it because I think my

readers will feel more at one with me. I would rather not publish it than let some publisher change it to suit themselves. Thankfully, my publishers got that, and I thank them for it. Therefore, you will undoubtedly see errors in the book, please don't blame the publisher… blame me!

At the point of completion, I needed two people to "read over it" and correct any obvious errors but not to change the character of the book. I needed people who were literate and someone who lived in Turkey to fact check my writing. These two people came in the shape of my sister, Kelly, who for most of her life I've labelled a geek because of her academic successes and a lady, called Sandra Yıldız, who lives in Marmaris and is happily married to a Turk.
I thank you both.

Please excuse any bad language, I couldn't express myself without it. I also ask that you read my book with an open mind and not judge me. They were definitely crazy times. I am far from perfect. I'm always open to criticism but please appreciate my writings are what I saw over the years with my own eyes. Opinions are my own and I went through hell to achieve those opinions. So, if you are one of these people who goes to Turkey three times a year and feel you are a professor of Turkish culture, then this book is probably not for you.

Turkish holiday resorts bear no resemblance to Turkish life or culture whatsoever! It's like saying a foreign holidaymaker that goes to Blackpool for the weekend knows Britain.

Special thanks to Marmaris Addiction. I couldn't have finished it without your support, guys.

Enjoy my story!

Paul Slaney

Contents

Prologue

After years pondering on when to start this book, I now discover I have another dilemma. Where? Having endlessly surfed the web looking for advice on how to write this autobiography it became apparent that I must take into consideration two factors before embarking on this crusade. The first one is easy, make a plan. Well, my plan, as you are about to discover, is to not have a plan!

My years of working in Turkey were just a catalogue of trials and tribulations and for this reason I'm going to stumble my way through it just as I did with everything from the very first day I arrived in this mysterious, beautiful country. In doing so I think you will appreciate that, as the saying goes, "the best laid plans of mice and men…" Turkey is a country where anything is possible, but these possibilities seem to unfold when you least expect them to.

The second factor I was told I had to take into consideration was a little less straight forward, "Which particular reader do I want to target?" This proves to be an even bigger dilemma. Obviously, visitors to Turkey would love to hear my story but so would many others as my journey involved other factors that, unfortunately, came with life in Turkey. Namely wine, women and song, to coin a phrase. However, as you are about to read, I wasn't only battling with life in a very strange country I also often came up against old friends like drink, women, depression and later, soft drugs. In a nutshell: I was the typical British stereotype who stumbled into the Turkish way of life and I hope you don't mind stumbling through it all again with me as I relive these last twelve years with you.

Now for the easy part, the thanks. Special thanks go to Denny, my partner in crime.
Hasan Acan and his brother Mehmet for taking me under their wing and guiding me through Turkish life in those first and most difficult couple of years.
Mikail and his brother Mehmet who saved my life on a couple of occasions and picked me up when I fell.
Finally, the good people of The Republic of Turkey who allowed me an insight into their culture and tolerated me for so long. I have only the greatest respect for the people of Turkey and in time, with much patience, the respect became mutual.
Lastly and more importantly I would like to thank that very special lady who, for the purpose of this book, we will call Sevil; not because it's one of the easier names to write but because in Turkish it means love and my love for her and for Turkey is what this book is all about.
I have had to protect some peoples' identities in this book, as I take you on my journey you will understand why.

I would like to dedicate this story to my family. I left a twelve-year gap in your lives and I thank you all from the bottom of my heart for allowing me to come back and be part of your lives again. Failing all else I hope that your children and your children's children will take pleasure in my autobiography for many years to come.

With Turkey attracting nearly four and a half million tourists every year it has become one of the top ten tourist destinations in the world and rightly so. For all of you who may be lucky enough to holiday in one of its many beautiful resorts you will find hospitality like you have never felt before. Turkey has something to offer everyone. Okay they may not be the most professional hosts you will find in the world. The sometimes "Fawlty Towers" way of going about things is part and parcel of a predominantly Muslim country trying so hard to cater for European tourists and to be honest it's what so many people love about Turkey and the Turkish way of life, me included. The sheer amateurishness of it all can either make you or break you and fortunately for the majority of holidaymakers who go to Turkey with a tongue in cheek attitude the whole experience can be one of bewilderment, disbelief and a joy to treasure.

Turkey has had her fair share of problems over the years with earthquakes and terrorist attacks, but this country just won't lie down. I have heard it said many times before that Turkey becomes another tourist destination that will go out of fashion. It hasn't and I don't think it ever will. Turkey, for some, is an addiction and for many of you reading this you will know where I'm coming from. Whether youngsters or pensioners it's a holiday that, for whatever reason, will stay in your memory for the rest of your life. So, what is it about Turkey that seems to hypnotize people? Well, there are many reasons and I'm sure when you reach the last page of this book I will have answered many of them. It seems no-one can put their fingers on it, unless of course you have witnessed what I have over the years. The more elderly folk tend to go for the hospitality. The Turks have so much respect for the elderly and quite simply can't do enough for them. Families go because Mum and Dad can relax knowing the Turks love for children will keep the kids amused and entertained. Youngsters love Turkey for the nightlife and the atmosphere and of course the ladies love it for the charming Turkish waiters with their boyish good looks and charm, which leads us to another reason for this book as I try to explain the infamous Turkish "Love Rats" syndrome. I could write a book on this extremely sensitive subject alone, but I have my theories and once again I hope I will be able to explain. Although many ladies out there might not like what they read I feel thousands more will take comfort from it.

You either love Turkey or hate it, there is not in between. I didn't only fall in love with the country I also fell in love with a beautiful Turkish woman. Little did I know at the time that first encounter on my very first night in Marmaris would change my life forever and after spending two brilliant weeks as a holidaymaker I would go back to a very different country as a worker.

I saw many come and go over the years quite simply because they couldn't hack working with the Turks, couldn't adapt into the culture and wanted to have their cake and eat it. You can't go to work in Turkey with an English mentality. If you want respect in Turkey, you have to earn it and to earn it you have to embrace the Turkish way of life and go with the flow. If you don't then I'm afraid you don't get to see the real Turkish life. For some this is a godsend because under the relaxing, laid back and warm exterior Turkey can quite simply swallow you up and spit you out in pieces.

1

The Land of Dodgy Mustaches and Carpets

February nineteen ninety-seven and, having just endured ninety minutes of being kicked from pillar to post by the opposition, I limped off the muddy pitch that Sunday morning cursing our team's performance to anyone that would listen. Our big centre half, Lee, was on the receiving end on this occasion.

"I'm chucking this Sunday morning football lark in," I moaned, albeit to no avail as he had heard it too many times before.

"Why should I get out of bed on a Sunday morning to play with this shower of shite," I went on. As I joined my girlfriend who was stood on the touchline, I turned to her for sympathy even though she knew nothing about football and had just come along to chat with Lee's wife about holidays.

"Did you see that bastard try to break my legs?" I asked her.

"No, we were looking at holiday brochures and we have decided on Turkey," she said… I knew it! The whole idea of my girlfriend turning out that bitterly cold February morning was to propose the idea of a holiday in Turkey that summer to me.

"No way am I going to Turkey," I proclaimed, "no bloody way, the land of dodgy mustaches and carpets? Bollocks to that," I continued.

"Tommy Cooper hats and kebabs? Not a chance!" An hour later we had gone back to Lee's house and out came the photographs of their previous year's holiday in Marmaris, Turkey. Reluctantly I flicked through them to find Lee in various states of drunkenness.

"Twenty pence a pint mate," he explained, "and that Raki stuff blows your sodding head off," he went on.

"Brought a couple of bottles back with me Paul fancies a glass?" he said reaching for the spirit cupboard. "Go on then after the morning I've had why not?" Two hours later and somewhat worse for wear, it was agreed, Turkey here we come! Who was I to argue anyway, the year before I had chosen Zante and it was the worst holiday we had ever had.

It seemed like an eternity waiting for the holiday to come along. At the time I worked in a fish house in Hull making fishcakes. Complete with wellies and hairnet I worked every hour possible to save up a decent amount of spending money. Now September was fast approaching and every day the thought of sunshine and beer at twenty pence a pint overcame the smell of fish that seemed to follow me everywhere I went. My girlfriend and I lived together, and the last few months were not particularly good ones. I had lost my father six months earlier and suffered a breakdown. Our relationship was strained and at breaking point. This holiday was, I suppose, make or break for us both. Lee and his wife pulled out of the holiday and were quickly replaced by my girlfriend's two brothers and partners, her mum and dad and another lad and his wife from our football team. So, in total there were ten of us, the more the merrier! Roll in September!

Going through Dalaman airport (who would have thought a few years later I would be getting marched through it at gunpoint) I was the typical stereotype Brit who was there to live it large. That long haul on the road to Marmaris that I now know so very well was a drag the halfway stop saw me and Phil, my girlfriend's brother, horrified to see a can of beer was actually a pound! But what the hell we were on holiday and a half hour later our coach pulled up to the Marmaris Sun Hotel (name changed). We all disembarked and were shown to our rooms. The long journey to Turkey had taken its toll and I was not impressed when I saw what we were expected to stay in for the next fourteen days. There was just enough room to swing a cat. What the hell we only wanted to sleep in it, and it was clean. After throwing our cases down we went to make our way downstairs to the bar for our first holiday drink when my girlfriend's mum called me to their room.
"Paul we can't sleep here," she exclaimed getting all upset. Rightly so, the double bed left them a few inches all round to get about.
"Right, that's it!" I snapped heading for the stairs.
"I'll get this sorted," I said firmly as I marched down the stairs to the reception area. I banged on the reception bell and waited; God help whoever came to that desk! Then, there she was, the receptionist. Her big brown eyes, her smile, her mere presence made my stomach do somersaults and it seemed an eternity before I could utter

something as my bottom jaw must have been touching the reception desk!
"Yes sir, can I help you?" she enquired. Her attempt at English only intensified the flame that was burning.
"Uh, uh," I was dumbstruck and probably for the first time in my life lost for words.
"It's my girlfriend's parents' room, would it be possible to change it please?" I asked politely, all my anger diminished by her presence, my eyes transfixed to her beautiful face.
"Of course, sir," she replied reaching up to the pigeon holes behind her for another key. She spoke in Turkish to the young boy behind the bar and handed him a key.
"Follow me sir," said the boy who had earlier helped us bring in our cases. I couldn't, my legs wouldn't move.
"Anything else sir?" the receptionist smiled.
"Uh no, thanks, that's great," I replied. As I followed the boy up the stairs and gave her one last look, she stared right back at me and gave me a smile, a different smile that went straight to my heart. I knew then, I don't know why but I knew at that moment I had just witnessed what had to be the most intense feeling in my life. Although I knew nothing about her, she was mine, she was my love. Great! Only been in Turkey five minutes and I had fallen in love with a Turkish woman and what's more I had my girlfriend with me!

Our first night was spent exploring, although my mind was on nothing else other than the receptionist. Having asked the hotel barman to recommend us a good place to eat we found ourselves in a Restaurant/Bar called Omar Sharif which was around a hundred yards from our hotel.

Within minutes we were getting acquainted with all the staff there. We had a thoroughly enjoyable night and, as you inevitably do on your first night on holiday, got wasted on the cheap local beer before wandering back to the hotel to try and catch up on some rest to be ready for our first full day in Turkey.

Boat trips, Turkish baths, Jeep Safaris, Turkish nights were all, explained our holiday rep, the "must do" things while we were in Turkey. To be honest I thought about nothing that next day while we were lazing around the pool. I would be quite happy if I never left the hotel grounds as from where I was laid, I had a perfect view of the receptionist and when our glances locked a smile always accompanied them. Was it me? Was I imagining things? Is it me she's smiling at or is there someone behind me?" I thought, glancing over my shoulder. No, it was definitely me! Maybe she smiles like that at all the customers, but she didn't, and I was in heaven and began to investigate further.

Our hotel barman was called Jacob, he is still a good friend to this day, and I will call him by his English name to avoid confusion. Yes, the Turks like to have English names and for whatever reason our barman had chosen Jacob as his. I have never been a sun worshiper it bores me to death so, having retired to the bar, I began to strike up a conversation with Jacob. I tried, without making it blatantly obvious, to find out more about the receptionist. To be honest I wish I had never mentioned Turkish women to him as he frightened me to bloody death!

"Paul don't even look at Turkish women, you will die," he explained in perfect English. Oh well, that was the end of that. However, during the course of the next couple of days, I did learn her name was Sevil, she was indeed married and had a small child… Oh fuck! Oh well the fantasy was nice while it lasted so I tried to put her out of my mind and enjoy the rest of our holiday. However, I couldn't and I found myself making excuses at every opportunity to go to the reception for my key. Every time I found Sevil looking deep into my eyes and that smile she gave me, oh that smile, she was driving me insane!

We still went in Omar's every night and had some great nights in there. I was made to feel particularly welcome by the manager whose name was Hasan. We would sit and talk for hours, and his English was excellent. On one particular night he challenged us to a game of football the following day. I rounded the lads up and we played the Omar Sharif staff in the ninety degrees Turkish midafternoon sun and got hammered! Hasan and myself hit it off straight away, he was a young shy lad but wanted to learn everything about England from me. His brothers, the still notorious twins "September and October", were probably the funniest pair I had ever met in my life. The owner of the bar and the elder brother Mehmet was a small, stocky intimidating figure and scared the living daylights out of me, but he always had a warm welcome for us in his somewhat different style of English language. We made some great friends in there and spent most of our holiday laughing and joking with the lads.

The holiday was flying by and it quickly became our second week. My encounters with Sevil became longer and more intimate and my girlfriend and her family were beginning to notice.

"Do you fancy that Turkish bird or what?" my girlfriend would ask jokingly. I brushed her accusations aside with amusement but the truth was I was in love and there was nothing in this world I could do about it! On the last few days we had booked for a few trips and this particular morning we had booked a boat trip so, while my girlfriend awoke enthusiastically packing our things, I had to find an excuse not to go.

"Think I ate something last night that didn't agree with me," I said rushing to the toilet, "my stomach is killing me." Probably due to the fact that I'd sunk 12 pints the night before and bought a kebab off the beach front.

"You're going to have to go without me," I said. After several minutes arguing about how much it had cost, my girlfriend packed her stuff and went to meet the rest of her family for the boat trip while I laid there thinking that if I was going to make a move it had to be today.

Thirty minutes later I was showered, dressed and sat in the morning sun having my first cup of coffee with a book which, apart from allowing me to hide behind, was of no interest to me whatsoever. For the first time I could freely observe Sevil as she worked, occasionally passing me, her perfume leaving a trail behind which told me this was indeed a very classy lady with expensive tastes. What did she see in a fish house worker from Hull? As usual she was immaculately dressed and her figure was complimented by her designer clothes. She wasn't the tallest of ladies but what she lacked in height she made up in beauty, her dark long wavy hair framed the most beautiful face I had ever seen. It was always painted in a way that just made me want to stare into those beautiful big brown eyes for an eternity. The way she gave out the orders to the staff it was quite obvious she was held in high regard at the hotel and it seemed that the staff both respected but also resented this woman telling them what to do. They muttered to each other when she gave them their morning duties.

I finished my second cup of coffee and retreated to the bar and began in earnest to chat with Oscar the daytime barman whilst still mesmerized by Sevil as she busied herself with her own jobs. She always looked over to me as if she wanted to talk but was a little shy. As I lifted myself up of the barstool and walked through the reception to the toilets I heard a voice call my name. There she was at the reception desk beckoning me over. I suppose looking back it was a little bit comical me with my pidgin Turkish and her with her poor English but that was the least of our worries. After a long and somewhat drawn-out attempt at conversation I discovered all I needed to know. Apart from looking into those eyes my eyes couldn't help taking glimpses at the amount of gold that adorned her ears and neck and again I asked myself the question, why me? I never did get to find out the reason even years later but that afternoon I was walking on air as she confirmed that the feelings I had for her were mutual and if you believe in love at first sight, well this was it in all its purity.

She was four years my junior at twenty eight years old, been married for two years and her child was a boy of six months. She was indeed the manager at the hotel and her husband was friends with the owner. She originated from Istanbul where her family still lived. She moved to Marmaris after her wedding and lived with her husband and his wealthy family. At this moment in time it wouldn't have mattered what her background was, I was infatuated! I was to find out in future months that not only did that day change my life it also changed hers in a way that was much more complicated than I could ever have imagined. I didn't understand a thing about Muslim life and to be honest I never wanted to, but as time went by I realised just how difficult a journey we had embarked on. The more I began to understand the Turkish culture the more scary it all became.

As I greeted the family back from the boat trip I was about to discover I had missed the best day of the holiday or so they thought. I sat at the bar listening to tails of Paradise Island and the many other places they stopped at. If only they had known I myself had been on a voyage that day but for me it was not over, there were many beautiful things I had yet to experience and many harrowing moments that lay undiscovered for now.

The last few nights sailed by and the days seemed like only minutes as myself and Sevil talked at every opportunity. She asked about my girlfriend, my children (I had two from my first marriage) and wanted to know if I would ever come back to Turkey. She explained that she wasn't happy in her marriage, she had felt under pressure to marry and have children. She had left it very late from the norm in Turkey to marry and have her first child and I could see the pain in her eyes as she explained her situation. I promised her I would return as soon as I sorted things out back in the UK but she would have to be patient as I just didn't know how long it would take. We didn't just discuss the obstacles in our way, we chatted generally too and she made me laugh so much, she had a great personality that also reflected on the other holidaymakers in our hotel, everyone seemed to have fallen in love with her.

One particular night we had booked a Turkish night at another hotel and apart from being probably the best night the family had witnessed in Turkey it was probably the best night for me and my future too because that night the barman in this hotel turned out to be the greatest friend I ever had in Turkey and someone who would be my mentor in Turkish life. His name was Yunus and he remains a great friend up until this day. Looking back now, he was the only person I could trust with regards to Sevil and he was always there for me when the sheer complexity of it all became too much for me.

The final day that I had been dreading since that very first night, arrived. We would be picked up early the next morning and this was our chance to go to Omar's and say our last goodbyes. I had hidden agendas. I wasn't thinking about it being my last night, indeed I was plotting my future. So for me this was a chance for me to tie up loose ends with regards to employment. I had discussed this with Hassan many times and it seemed there was a job waiting for me the following season. I suppose looking back he, as I have since, had heard it many times in drunken conversations from many holidaymakers before.

I, however, had a good reason to return and as we finished what would be our last dinner together at Omar's that season Sevil walked into the restaurant with a Turkish friend. Mehmet (the boss) looked on in bewilderment as it's extremely rare to see a Turkish woman in restaurant catering for Europeans. There she was and all of a sudden it was starting to look way too obvious to the people around me. However, as I was later to discover, my girlfriend was indeed occupied with her own hidden agenda so seeing Sevil come into the restaurant didn't phase her one bit. I suppose from the moment when I danced with her my future boss knew why I wanted to come back to Turkey. I think he could see it, I think everyone could but the truth of it all was when I took her in my arms for that first dance I didn't care. I didn't care one bit, she was my world and nothing, but nothing, was going to come between us. As we left Omar's that night and did the usual "see you next year" bit I assured the lads I would be back in a few weeks. As we exchanged telephone numbers I don't think they appreciated how serious I really was.

The next morning I awoke knowing this was going to be one of the most difficult days of my life and as the coach arrived to take us to the airport I could never have imagined how much of an understatement that was. All packed and ready to go we said our last goodbyes to the hotel staff. Trying to hold back my emotion I saved Sevil until the last and fighting back the tears I held her and whispered my intentions into her ear. "I will see you soon darling," I choked.

"Paul promise me," she whispered back, "promise me," as she slipped something into my hand.
"I promise you Sevil," I said.
"Please don't be long Paul," she pleaded and as we separated and I took one last look into those eyes I could see that I wasn't the only one going through all that pain that fine summer morning. The engine started and as we waved our farewells I opened my clenched fist to find her bracelet. That very bracelet never left my hand until I returned a couple of weeks later. The journey home was dreadful I felt I was leaving part of me there and arriving back in Hull it seemed like a fairytale had ended. I was determined there was nothing going to take it away from me though and the next few days I was in a self-imposed trance with my mind on one thing and one thing only. How and when would I get back?

A week after our return, with normality apparently setting in for everyone but myself, I found a letter hidden away in our bedroom. It was addressed to Mithat, one of the waiters at Omar's. It was from my girlfriend stating her affections for him and that the kiss they had was special, as I read further with disbelief it went on to say that she couldn't stop thinking about him and that she hoped they could stay friends and maybe more. Her last sentence put the final nail in our coffin when she pleaded with him not to mention it to any of the other staff in the restaurant as if Paul found out he would be very angry and, hypocritically I know, I did feel angry. When I confronted her with the letter she dismissed it as just a silly spur of the moment thing and that she was never going to send the letter. For me it was conclusive though, we were over and un-reconcilable. That "make or break holiday" had indeed broke us, but in a selfish way she had eased my own conscience and that made me even more determined to get back to Turkey.

Two days later having taken my wages out of the bank I decided I was going to simply disappear and not tell anyone. Not my girlfriend, family or my boss at the fish house. After calling Hasan at the restaurant and telling him I would be coming back he was absolutely delighted and told me he would pick me up from Dalaman airport. The following week saw me waiting in Manchester airport for my flight. I didn't need to book a hotel as Hassan had booked me into an apartment across the road from Omar's. Only two people knew I would be arriving at Dalaman in those early hours of that October morning, Hasan and Sevil. She didn't believe it and if the truth be known, I was having trouble comprehending the fact as well, even as those tyres screeched on landing on the runway at Dalaman.
True to his word Hasan was waiting with open arms as I walked through the airport doors and it appeared most of the staff from Omar's had driven the hour and a half through the night with him to pick me up. That just confirmed to me how genuine and sincere this family really was.

As we drove through Marmaris it seemed like a ghost town. 4am in the morning and not a holidaymaker in sight. It made me realise that the end of the season was fast approaching and Marmaris was winding down. As we arrived at my apartment I bid all goodnight and I would see them early in the morning. However the rest of the night saw me sat on my balcony watching Marmaris wake up and listening to the now all to familiar sound of shop shutters being rolled up and a few late night drunken revelers struggling to find their way back to their hotels.

"Paul Ne haber lan pust," came the greeting from the boss as I walked into Omar's that morning. He basically gave me a slang Turkish greeting in his own unique style that I was to emulate for many years to come. Mehmet (the boss) spoke little English but his way of phrasing things even in Turkish made me understand what he wanted to say. That particular morning as I sat drinking coffee with him he seemed more interested in his newspaper than his future employee, but that was Mehmet all over. He was a man that demanded respect and got it from everyone including myself for many years to come. I could wait no longer and after being grilled by everyone as to where I was going I made my way down to the Marmaris Sun Hotel. With a look of both confusion and glee Jacob greeted me like a long-lost brother "Paul, what are you doing back here?" he asked "Where are the rest of the family?" he enquired further. If I was clever I should have known these questions were going to have to be answered but I hadn't anticipated it so I found myself avoiding them until I could think of a reason why I would be back in Marmaris by myself. It was while we were sat chatting in the early morning sunshine that she appeared. She just stood there smiling, if only I could have run up to her and held her and let my emotions pour out. Alas this wasn't possible. No-one could know what was going on between us. It was far too dangerous, not only for me but particularly for her. So as she approached my table and shook my hand I just had to read her eyes and in any language they told me all I needed to know.

That one week was going to be the shortest week of my life and luckily for us with the season winding down we had plenty of time for, albeit somewhat incomprehensible, conversation and sneaky kisses. We did manage to overcome the language barrier sometimes as I spoke in child like English but most of my inquisitions were met with the same answer, "Paul I no understand," It was making me crazy with frustration that I couldn't make her understand my feelings and I needed help from someone, but who could I trust? The answer was right in front of my eyes. I just didn't know it at the time.

My days were spent hiding from the sun. (Well, I couldn't really go back to rain sodden Hull with a suntan could I?). I would spend my time both at Omar's and Sevil's hotel. One particular night when I walked into her hotel I just felt something was wrong as the atmosphere was solemn.

"What's wrong with everyone?" I asked the Barman whose name was Tuncay.

"Paul it's Sevil, she will divorce from her husband," he said reaching for a bottle of whisky under the bar, "tonight I will be very drunk," he exclaimed.

"Paul for Muslim women divorce is terrible," he went on. So what's the big deal I thought, it happens in the UK everyday. In my defense my ignorance meant I knew nothing else. However, as I later discovered, for a Muslim woman to divorce is indeed unthinkable. She would be in all effect an outcast for the rest of her life. She would now be considered "used goods" for want of a better word and no true Muslim man wants a divorced woman especially one with a young child. Sevil had explained her situation to me, how her husband's family ran her life, once again my ignorance led me to believe she was a victim here when in actual fact it is normal in such circumstances for the husband's family to have control over what goes on.

It wasn't all doom and gloom though and my nights were spent either in Sevil's hotel or indeed Omar's where she would turn up accompanied by her hotel guests using them as both an excuse and an alibi. Mehmet would always greet her into his restaurant and then give me a smile as if to say he knew what was going on. Mehmet never missed a trick and as times went by he was always there for me if I needed advice. Although blunt and straight to the point, which was Mehmet all over, he was always on hand and in later months would encourage me to come clean about the whole thing. I couldn't though, not in Marmaris. The few Turks who live there in winter all knew each other's business and rumors went around like a bush fire, it was way too dangerous. If her husband found out before or even after their divorce then he could possibly stop her seeing her child ever again. We needed time alone and we got it one particular night as we had arranged to go to İçmeler, a place a couple of miles outside of Marmaris. We had it all planned, we would both wait for the bus (dolmuş) separately and then once in İçmeler when it was less likely we would be spotted, we could relax a little. Having spruced up I found myself in the Mimosa hotel drinking Raki for a bit of Dutch courage. My friend Yunus was also pleased to see me back but he was also puzzled as to why I had come back alone.

I don't know why, but I trusted Yunus from the start and as I sat there talking with him at the bar I found myself committing the immortal sin of telling him everything! At first he didn't believe me but Yunus was a very modern Turk who was merely working in his friend's bar to subsidise his University fees. He was twenty four years old and his perfect English suggested he had been very well educated.
"Paul Turkish women are difficult," he smiled. After finishing downing my fourth Raki and informing him of my date on the front he took me by the arm and told me if I needed help I knew where to find him.

As agreed, that night Sevil and I stood at the bus stop ten metres apart and on the bus sat quietly smiling at each other from our respective seats. Once in İçmeler we were free and walked the beach hand in hand before eating together and finally making our way back to Marmaris and the secrecy and frustration. That night was amazing and I wanted to tell the world! I couldn't and wouldn't be able to for a long time to come.

I saw two very different sides to Sevil that week, the very serious and disciplined way she went about her job and with her staff and also the bubbly young lady who made me laugh with her almost European attitude in wanting to have fun. She was cheeky, sarcastic and the life and soul of a party in order to entertain her hotel guests yet strong, self standing and extremely ambitious, a trait that I came to learn was typical of the Turkish culture. I also had a close encounter with her husband one night whilst sat at the bar in her hotel when he actually walked in and sat next to me. Thinking I was a guest he enquired as to where I was from etc., I couldn't help but notice his hand was bandaged and not having the courage to ask how it had happened all sorts of things were racing through my mind. I quickly made my exit and the following day was informed by Sevil that he had done it fighting! Brilliant I thought just bloody brilliant!

The last day was fast approaching and it was whilst in conversation with Yunus, venting my frustration out on him that he came up with a suggestion that was the answer to all my problems. His hotel had very few guests in it now, it was quiet, dark and perfectly situated at the end of a cul de sac.

"Paul, meet her here and I will translate for you both," he said, finding obvious pleasure in his solution to our problem. That was it, the answer, I could finally spill out my heart to her albeit through a translator. There was one problem though How the hell would I tell her Yunus knew everything about us? Putting the suggestion to her that day was a bit nerve racking but surprisingly she agreed. I think through sheer frustration herself and she told me to pass on her number to Yunus so the rendezvous could be organised. Everything was arranged for the following evening, she would meet me at the Mimosa. I remember that night as if it was yesterday, I sat there patiently waiting for her to turn up. When she eventually did, she came accompanied by her little boy in his pushchair and as we all sat down opposite each other Yunus positioned himself at the end of the table and in the middle. This was my opportunity to let off steam and I wasn't going to waste it and it appeared Sevil had the

same thoughts. As we explained our feelings for each other both our eyes welled with tears of joy, we could finally make our feelings known to each other. I wasn't looking at Yunus only into her eyes and was surprised that my translator had not repeated my one particular statement. I turned to look at him as if to prompt him. Yunus wasn't there. Where was he?
"Paul I can't do this anymore," a sobbing voice came from under the table, "it's all too much for me," he said clambering up onto his chair.

Fortunately that was the first and the last time we would need a translator.
Yunus and I had many reasons to laugh and cry as we became closer in the following years but looking back to that night I smile to myself. Funny as the situation was Yunus took a lot of weight off our shoulders and we all left the hotel that night happy. Happy because myself and Sevil had got everything off our chests and I'm sure Yunus was happy that it was all over, although he did later explain later that he had never heard anything so emotional in his life. We also had someone we could trust with regards to our relationship and Sevil would often call Yunus when she didn't understand my typically English way of going about things.

I will spare you the details of what would turn out to be my last day in Marmaris as a holidaymaker as I feel I have accomplished what I wanted to do in this opening chapter, which was to explain my reasons for going to Turkey; my love affair with a Turkish woman. The remainder of the book will explain how I fell in love with Turkey itself.

I could feel the October chill as I moved slowly forward in that endless queue waiting to check in for my return back home. Various cancellations meant that the end of the queue was well outside the airport doors and onto the car park. Chinese whispers filtered down the line with regards to the length of delays expected. I reached into my pockets to check my tickets only to find I had lost my wallet somewhere along with its contents: tickets, cards, money etc. and all of a sudden it didn't seem so cold as panic struck. What could I do? Stuck at the airport in a foreign country without a penny. As panic was setting in I felt a tap on my shoulder. It was the cook at Omar's, they had driven all the way back to Marmaris found my wallet on the back seat and he drove the one and a half hours back to Dalaman with it! Talk about a relief! After a two hour delay I boarded my plane and never once thought about what sort of a reception I would get when I returned back home. My only thoughts were related to my plans to return the following April for the whole season. It was only as I got back to the UK and onto my coach to Hull I had to address the issue of my return and I wondered if I could slip into Hull as easily as I had slipped out. I did so with relative ease that suggested how little effect I actually had on peoples lives.

At the time I was playing with a band and we used to practice upstairs in a local pub in Hull. It's where I first met Karl, the landlord, and we became good friends. It was he who suggested I stay with him for a while until I got myself sorted as I obviously couldn't go back to my girlfriend's house. As luck would have it I met an ex work colleague in the pub that Sunday afternoon who offered me a place to stay and after collecting the rest of my things from my girlfriend's house without too much fuss, I settled in for a very cold and long winter without work as I had been inevitably sacked from the fish house. I didn't care though. I didn't care about anything. I was focused on April and April alone.

Letters from Sevil would arrive at Karl's pub and with excitement I would open them and scan through page after page of meaningless text. Today with the aid of mobiles and e-mails letters can be sent worldwide in seconds. Back in the late nineties we didn't have that luxury and letters would take anything between three weeks and well, never, getting to you. When my first letter did arrive I found myself buying a dictionary thinking I could translate the letters with relevant ease. Impossible! I laugh when I see people trying it today. Turkish is not a language that is written as it's spoken and therefore trying to translate direct from a dictionary is like pissing into the wind but God how I tried and came up with many, many conclusions as to the contents of her letters. My room was like a detectives' incident room with endless scenarios as to what each word actually meant. However once again lady luck shone on me. It was brought to my attention that an old Turk was a regular in the pub and so the agreement was I bought his beer and he translated my letters. I was relieved that her correspondence actually coincided with mine which meant she too had found herself an interpreter. Chef, the old Turk, was from

Istanbul. He would invite me around to his house to join him and the rest of Hull's Turkish community in a regular game of cards, Turkish coffee, Turkish snacks and of course Raki. I learned a lot on those nights, most of all how the Turks hated losing!

Christmas came and went and we were finally into nineteen ninety eight. Unbeknown to me it was going to be the best year of my life. I had eventually found a job bagging sawdust in a local wood yard. Nothing to write home about but that job enabled me to save and apart from the odd night out, I was happy just to sit and wait until summer arrived. Sevil did call me when she got the chance. She was now in Istanbul with her mother but our telephone conversations were, let's say, short, with me asking her how she was and she saying she was fine and that she loved me and basically that's about all the language barrier allowed. One particular Sunday morning when she called, I was playing football and Linda, my work colleague and temporary landlady, answered the phone. She explained that I was out. When Sevil called back later she wanted to know why a woman had picked up the phone and wasn't happy at all about it.

Life went on as normal for most people around me and although I did mention my intentions to close friends and family the thought of me leaving Hull for Turkey was just met with patronizing smiles. However I kept going and the letters I received from Hassan confirming my job offer just added fuel to my fire.

Hull is a strange place as everyone seems to hate the place but no-one seems to actually leave it. Except one Paul

Slaney who was sat excitedly waiting for my bus to Manchester airport and to a place that would change my life forever. So with my friends and family still not completely convinced of my intentions, I was gone. Everyone expected this pipe dream to be over in a couple of weeks and see me return home with my tail between my legs, how little they knew.

2

That Crazy Hazy First Summer

Late April and I arrived in Marmaris on the first holiday flight to Dalaman armed with three suitcases which seemed to amuse the lads as they packed them into their white Fiat rental car. When we arrived in Marmaris I couldn't believe how quiet it was. The only people around were reps, locals and builders hastily putting the finishing touches to restaurants desperate to complete alterations ready for the season to open on May the first. Once again my flight had included a local hotel for a fortnight so I still had the security of accommodation and a return flight home a fortnight later should everything go wrong. Having unpacked and made my way to Omar's I was greeted by the staff and of course the boss who still didn't seem impressed by me being there.

"Oh Paul Ne Haber Lan Ibne," he shouted from behind his newspaper. I don't know why but Mehmet scared the living daylights out of me, as he did most people. Behind his rhetoric when, in Turkish, he would call me a pimp, a homosexual, and a dog amongst other things he was a man who I still have great respect for and for all his faults there is no-one in Turkey who I would rather have had as my first boss. He was the eldest of four brothers and owned the restaurant. Short and stocky with a neat beard and a bald head he looked like your typical gangster boss. He was thirty eight years of age and without a wife and children. He had three brothers in Turkey, Hasan and the twins Halit and Hatar (known as September and October). They also had Omar Sharif who the restaurant was named after, he had originally worked in Marmaris, married an English woman and now lived in South Yorkshire. The family were of Arabic origin and, as I was to discover later, the family, apart from Mehmet and Hasan, were devout Muslims who lived in Izmir in the winter and returned to Marmaris for the summer as most businessmen do. In fact the population in Marmaris was minimal in the winter and as the season opened people would arrive from every corner of Turkey but that particular season few had traveled as far as I did to work, apart from holiday reps whom, particularly Airtours and Sunquest, I was to form some close friendships with.

It appeared I had arrived before anyone I knew. The staff at Omar's had been there a couple of weeks cleaning but apart from that both Yunus and more importantly Sevil would arrive later. I was rather bemused when I asked Hasan when I would start work and what I would be doing. I was told to take a holiday and I would start when the holidaymakers arrived. The truth is I wanted to be part of it, I wanted to clean the restaurant and be treated like I was part of the team, what else could I do? I knew no-one apart from the lads in the restaurant, so after walking around Marmaris every day it appeared we were not the only restaurant not quite ready for the opening day of the season. They were all in the process of getting ready to open, including the staff at Sevil's hotel, The Marmaris Sun.

Opening day of the season 97 and just look at the weather!
September, myself, Sado, Steven and October. Our chef in the front

My favourite Turkish bar and the effects of
cheap Raki and Turkish music

Paul's crazy karaoke corner at Omar Shariff

3am in Omars, myself and Mico entertaining customers

Myself and my old friend Mehmet in River Jewellery

I would often sit with Mustafa, the owner, drinking Raki as he sat there all day supervising his staff on how to clean a swimming pool properly. It was quiet times like this that allowed me to evaluate the team I was to be working with that season. A team that would eventually see us become one of the best and busiest restaurants in Marmaris. We all had our own individual characters and seeing the arrival from Antalya of our head waiter Micho the team was complete. The Chef (Nehad) was from Izmir and for all his personality faults was a genius in the kitchen. Hot headed though he was, he ran our kitchen with military precision, his brother, who was the second chef, I hated with a vengeance. Sado the crazy kurdish Pizza chef who resembled a PKK activist was, in fact, a kid I had a great deal of time for. Then the waiters Halit and Hatar (September and October). The terrible twins and terrible they were to a point where I could have killed them both but at nineteen years old they were the funniest double act I have ever seen in my life. They have both grown up a lot now and I'm sure there are people reading this who may know them both and just their names will make you smile. If truth be known behind the scenes they broke my heart many times but equally they had me in stitches with some of their antics. Fanatic Muslims though they were, without a doubt these two made many of our customers come back year after year. Steven (Mehmet), a Kurdish waiter who I watched grow from a boy to a man, was like my little brother. I spent many an afternoon teaching him English and in time this fearless Kurd was to watch my back and stand by me when the shit hit the fan. Yelcin was our hassle man and the one we all relied on to bring in the customers. He originated from Marmaris, indeed his family were very rich. However, after a jet ski accident in İçmeler a few years prior, he was left let's say "a little crazy" and definitely one you wouldn't want to get on the wrong side of. He was renowned in Marmaris for his ability to fight and although we had few major disagreements, I knew people stayed away from our restaurant because of his creepy, weird and sometimes deeply insulting attitude towards customers. I liked Yelcin, an old school hassle man. He spoke every language under the sun and I was to learn a lot from him in time to come. Hasan, the assistant manager and my mentor in the restaurant, is the one person who, with his perfect English, I could always turn to when I didn't agree with something. As he was the boss's brother, I always seemed to get my point across. A semi pro footballer in Izmir, Hassan was twenty four, had a modern mentality and just soaked up the many lessons I gave him on the English language and culture. I must add he always had time to give me a Turkish lesson in exchange. Hasan, for a resort worker, was extremely shy and still is today. I have fond memories of some great times we spent together. Then there was Micho (another Mehmet) who was to be the head waiter. A big handsome Turk who although had an eye for the ladies (you would call him our love rat) he went about his job in a thoroughly professional manor and as he and our Chef had previously worked together the understanding between himself and the kitchen staff was perfect! So to our boss (Mehmet) our leader: terrible English, some strange ways of going about things but someone you always knew would be there for you in good times and bad. One for the ladies, our boss was a larger-than-life character and although we all used to call him behind his back, he was a caring man, a loyal man and a man that eventually opened up his arms and allowed me into his family like his own brother. Last but not least, this Englishman who had turned up out of the blue to work with the Omar Sharif team. What was his job here? Well that Friday morning I was about to find out!

"Paul, holiday finished," came a voice from the cashier's desk as the boss folded up his beloved paper and slammed it on the desk. With this, Hasan explained my job description. I was Omar Sharif's official barman which was no problem for me as I had worked for many years as a relief manager for Vaux Inns, however that was the UK and this is Turkey so I listened carefully as Hasan explained things. With only one beer pump and a fridge full of bottles to look after this was like taking candy from a baby I thought. Although sixteen hours a day, seven days a week with no holiday, the massive thirty pounds a week I would be paid seemed to compensate for those miserable working hours! To be honest the salary wasn't my motivation, far from it. My plan was to keep my head down, prove what I was capable of and learn the culture for the sake of mine and Sevil's future. As I stood familiarizing myself with my new work environment the tourists came in their hordes down our street and towards the Friday market from which Omar's was only a stone's throw away. I could hear every hassle man's attempts to lure the crowds into their respective establishments but our position opposite the traffic lights gave our own hassle man, Yelcin, a chance to turn on his own banter.
"Cold drinks, English breakfast, snacks," he shouted but failed to pull in the pale skinned holidaymakers eager to

make it past the constant stream of hassle before being swallowed up by the hustle and bustle of Marmaris market. Still awaiting my first rush I looked on with amusement. I was told the season had started.
"Is this it?" I thought, cleaning my bar of the few drips left behind from the couple of beers I had pulled. If only I knew that after the tourists' confrontation with what has to be one of the most hectic markets in the world they would come armed with carrier bags full of junk into the nearest watering holes, one of them being Omar Sharif's!
Armed only with a kettle, eight cups, a box of sugar cubes and a few spoons I tried to fend off the requests from the waiters who where getting flustered themselves as they threw endless pieces of paper onto the bar with the customers orders and table number. I quickly had to learn how to count to ten in Turkish as the waiters reconfirmed their orders to me in Turkish and my only break came when someone actually ordered a beer! Fresh Orange juice was a nightmare too because all we had was one of those hand pull contraptions and depending on the amount of juice in the oranges could take up to five minutes to make a pint! I have to admit I got my English face well and truly bloodied that long, hot Friday and although I did go under at times there was Hasan to help me out and by four o'clock after six hours non stop it was over!
"Paul this is the first week of the season," explained Hasan. "This is nothing compared to high season," he said whilst helping me clean the ransacked bar. I learned many valuable lessons that day as I crawled the short distance back to my apartment. Amongst them I had

learned how to say tea, coffee and orange juice in Turkish and how to count from one to ten.
I learned to hate Fridays for the rest of my working life in Turkey, and most of all I learned that the Turks like to make things difficult for themselves by only preparing things last minute and facing the inevitable consequences later. I was to change this over the next few weeks. As I lay on my soft pillow in my apartment the gentle breeze of the fan cooling me down and satisfied that I had pulled through my first day, I realised it had slipped my mind to ask the boss about accommodation. My two weeks stay was just about up in my holiday apartment, never mind I would ask him that evening I thought as I drifted off to sleep.

Six o'clock and I was showered, dressed and making my way back to the restaurant where I was met by my boss. He was not happy at all. Apparently the waiters were late for work and I was instructed to go and get them at our staff living quarters close by. When I knocked on the door of this small brown shed-like building I was greeted by Steven who explained they would be there shortly as they had no hot water. I stood there in silence stunned at the sight that lay before me. I could have packed my bags and gone home there and then. A small room barely big enough to squeeze the two triple tier bunk beds in and one toilet/shower to be shared by all six of our staff for the whole summer! Any self satisfaction I had of my efforts that day were quickly replaced by fear.
"Surely they can't expect me to live like this" I thought as I walked back up the street and into our restaurant. Having re-stocked my bar for the night I sat down with

the boss and explained my situation. He put my mind at rest assuring me he had somewhere for me to stay. As I finished a quiet shift on the bar Yelcin explained that I would move into his apartment the next day and to come with my cases early in the morning. The next morning arrived and a couple of the lads helped me haul my cases up the four flights of stairs to the top floor where my room for the summer awaited me. You can't imagine what was going through my mind as the door opened. I couldn't help but wish I was a holidaymaker again. A room ten foot by eight with two iron beds greeted me, with no windows the morning sun was already making its presence felt as I reluctantly walked in.

"Oh well when in Rome" I thought unpacking my clothes and folding them up neatly on the newspaper that lay at the foot of my bed. At least I had a place I could call my own I thought until I inquired as to the whereabouts of the mattress. "The Cook is bringing them," said Yelcin. Them? He went on to say I would be sharing my box with our Cook. As he closed the door on me I sat on the bed and seriously contemplated going home.

"Surely they can't expect me to live here," I thought, "are they taking the piss?" I stopped unpacking and went on to the landing to the bathroom that I was to share with four others who lived on the top floor. It was disgusting and pulling back the filthy shower curtain I wondered how the hell I would bring myself to make this my home for the whole summer.

"Oh by the way Paul," exclaimed Yelcin about to descend the stairs. "My grandmother sleeps on the third floor and you will have to walk through her bedroom on a night so please try and keep the noise down." That little room saw every emotion possible from me that season and be it tears of laughter or sadness those tears quickly dried up as the temperature in there reached as high as one hundred and thirty degrees in the Marmaris midday heat!

The following weeks saw me settling in and also saw me take control of my little bar. The endless array of cocktails we offered, which looked daunting at first, soon became my specialty and although not quite yet Tom Cruise I was getting there. I found myself responsible for my own stock and even learned how to negotiate prices with the orange sellers who arrived on a daily basis in lorries laden with loose Oranges. "Paul, Oranges?" they would ask in Turkish obviously thinking I was an easy touch. Little did they know I had been taught by the boss himself how to select only the finest oranges that could produce the most juice and increase out profit margin. I would take an orange from every part of the lorry and cut them open, taste them and then squeeze them. Only when I was satisfied with the quality and the price would I go ahead and buy. After much haggling I usually got a good price and all our staff would sit happily eating the free samples. Ice also was a major dilemma, order too little and we could not serve cold cocktails order too much and the ice, although kept in freezers, would simply defrost. It was a fine balance but one of the duties I had to get just right in order to progress. When I wasn't working behind the bar I had other jobs to tend to. These were mainly writing signs, posters and menus. If it needed writing in English I was the man for the job, not just in our restaurant but also for the boss's friends who would reward me with a beer or two.

Omar's was situated on a roundabout and on each corner of the street stood our competition. George and Dragon on one side, Prestige on the opposite side and the notorious Simpson's on the other side. In fact we had many other restaurants to compete with Paradise, Mr. Cooks, No limit, and Al Pacino's to name a few. When I say competition I mean it, as in win at all costs competition. We never spoke to anyone from other restaurants only Queen's Chinese, Faulty Towers and Prestige were considered our friends because the owners or the staff were friends of ours. We frequently borrowed/lent high chairs, ice, beer and spirits to each other. I had taken my bar job by the horns within three weeks of the season's start and Fridays, although still a major ball ache, I made it easier by simply getting the boss to invest in more cups and a huge water boiler. I also had one of the lads squeeze all the oranges the night before and put the juice into huge plastic cartons. The lads had taken to me and I would sit and listen to their idle chit chat half in English for my benefit and half in Turkish depending on who was present. I began to feel like I was part of the team and to them I wasn't a holidaymaker anymore. I was one of them and I was needed. I also enjoyed sitting with the Brits when I had finished my stint at the bar and I spent many a late night with customers who later became good friends.

People have this strange notion that Turkey has a relaxed attitude towards timekeeping and I'm sure all of you who know resort workers well are aware that the working hours are set like clockwork, there is no excuse for lateness or illness. My hours were from nine in the morning for breakfast service until two in the afternoon and then I would begin again at six in the evening and work through until one or two in the morning. For Turks that's normal but for me working in blistering heat in the day used to take its toll and as much as I would have loved to have slept in my afternoon break, the woman who I came for wanted my attention too. By five minutes past two I would be sat at the reception of her hotel making conversation with Sevil which was now getting a lot easier. Sevil's English was getting better due to the amount of Brits she had staying in her hotel. My Turkish was still very limited but, thanks to the lads in Omar's, I was starting to understand, not only vocabulary, but the body language that plays a very important part of the Turkish language. I would also pay Yunus a visit twice a week and although we were both too busy to make a night of it we would talk for ages at his hotel. I think the jacket potatoes and chili they served was my staple diet for what seemed like weeks. Around four o'clock I would head back to my little top floor oven for a couple of hours siesta. However, especially in high season, it was just impossible to sleep and I would lay there literally dripping with sweat. That is one of the reasons I got in to drinking a small bottle of Raki before I slept. It was my night nurse.

The other reason I started drinking Raki was for Dutch courage, as after only a month of being a barman I was about to climb to the top of the ladder and become a hassle man, a job that is considered to be the top job and it's the highest paid in the resorts. I will explain the Turks unique system of working later and in depth as this for me is the main reason why Turkey has become one of the leaders in foreign holidays. It also explains why hassling women is not only for sex, there are hidden agendas and this subject warrants its own chapter. For me, although I didn't know it at the time, it was as high as you go as a resort worker. It came about for me one day when our hassle man Yelcin fell sick. The boss pulled me over and finally paid me the money he owed me from the start of the season. I had been asking him for some time for my wages as my debts were quickly mounting up, both at Sevil's and Yunus's hotels. As the boss seemed to be happy to part with the lira, which for any Turkish boss is highly unusual, I was puzzled. "Paul I need you to hassle tonight?" the boss said. After refusing point blank and telling him I didn't have the guts to do it, he opened a bottle of his own finest Malt whiskey and poured us both a glass.

"Only one night, maybe two," he assured me. Sure enough three large malts later I was outside on the street hassling for all I was worth. For me it was easy, see an English family walking up the street ask them where they were from and then they would stop and chat. They would be relieved, after running the gauntlet of the hard hassles down our street, that they had come across an Englishman who didn't want to hassle them. Just have a chat and give out some information. Inevitably they would come in and by the end of the night I had filled the restaurant and become a hero in the eyes of my work colleagues. Okay I slipped up sometimes when I tried to hassle people from other countries and found out I couldn't speak their respective language but with eighty percent of tourists in Marmaris being Brits I was an instant success. As I explained, there is a very good reason for hard hassle in Turkey. Although I have never for one minute understood the logic behind the reasoning of why a hassle man in Turkish resorts is held in the highest esteem by Turkish bosses, let's just say for the moment it's him who is responsible for getting people into the restaurant/bar and making money, not only for the boss and staff but for their families back home as well.

I never did go back behind my bar again, I was too important for that now but little did I know at the time I was getting noticed and putting myself in the limelight by making Omar's full every night. For me, especially being an Englishman, drawing attention to myself was not a good idea as it brought out the one trait I was to hate most about Turkey…jealousy, intense jealousy. I was pulling in the punters and other restaurants didn't like it.

There are two things that you should never interfere with in Turkey, a Turkish man's woman and a Turkish man's money. I was to do both in the coming months and I paid a price for it. Fortunately I had a well connected boss otherwise the price could have been much, much higher.
It's very rare for any workers in Turkey to go far from their restaurant and I was no exception. Most restaurants have their own form of transport for the staff's convenience whether it be a car a scooter or in our case a bicycle. It's very rare to see a Turk walking in the red-hot sun. In the high season it can make a walk of a mile seem like ten and in those early days I can count the times I left a distance of hundred yards in diameter of Omar's on one hand. When I did, I walked and although at times I

needed that space to breathe a little I couldn't, there was always someone wanting to chaperone me and it could get quite embarrassing. It's perfectly normal to see Turkish friends walk arm in arm down the street and although I know it looks a bit dodgy it's not. Unless you're a tourist of course then obviously it looks extremely iffy. So when I walked down the main street of Marmaris on my way to buy yet more fluorescent paper and felt tip pens for yet more posters, I always had one of our lads arms around me. It's what the Turks do, that touchy feely thing and after repeatedly politely requesting them not to do it to no avail, I ended up giving up. Even while sat in the restaurant talking the lads would quite innocently have a hand on my knee, it's a habit of theirs and one that means that you are a close friend however to some people it definitely looks more.

One place I religiously went was to watch the local football team Marmarispor. I went with my boss on the back of his scooter. So after purchasing his pistachio nuts we would go through the turnstiles to an atmosphere you could never find in any football stadium in Britain and this was just a small first division club. For a neutral it just had to be witnessed as five thousand Turks went berserk for ninety minutes. My boss calmly walked into the stadium and just like the red sea parted for Moses, the crowd parted for him to take his seat. He then turned into a lunatic himself as he bayed for the blood of the opposition.

Late night Karaoke with the staff and Airtours reps

Kiss Kiss on the bar on a Friday afternoon, as you do in Turkey

My Dad, Mam, Steven and Hasan with customers

Myself and Yunus drunk in Greenhouse

Later I was to take our customers to see Marmarispor as I thought any genuine football fan would just relish this euphoria… and they did. I enjoyed those matches not only as it was an eye opener but also because it gave me time away from Omar's as well as quality time with my boss. I think in that first season I had, in total, two days off. One because I had taken in too much sun and was sick, the other was one morning when I skived off for the day.

Sevil had called Omar's, as she did most mornings, and I wasn't there. On the spur of the moment she decided she wanted to go on a boat trip with me so she was given Yelcin's number and he woke me up. I had to be on the beach front within fifteen minutes! Five minutes later saw me running the entire length of the beach to catch the boat and off we went on what turned out to be an amazing day however on my return there seemed a lot of grim faces and for the first time I got a real rollicking off the boss. I don't think it was because I had taken a day off without telling him but more because he was concerned for my safety. He wanted to know where I was every minute of the day for my own safety. I later told him where I had been and who with and he calmed down because Sevil was not only important to me but was very important for Omar's.

The Turks rely heavily on friends working in hotels to recommend a good restaurant to their guests. Although it's strictly forbidden by the hoteliers it does go on and we used to get a lot of business from Sevil's hotel guests. She was the one person my boss wanted to keep on the right side of. Holiday reps too were girls it was best to keep on the right side off. Although it was not in the holiday company's regulations to recommend places, a discount on their meals always used to get them recommending Omar's. It was also my job to keep the reps happy, so I used to have many a morning chit chat with the girls from Airtours and Sunquest over a cup of tea as they set about their daily routines.

So here I was two months into the season and everything was going to plan. I was the main man in Omar's now and my hassling job was made easier now the high season was coming on. A full restaurant every night has a knock-on effect as tourists see it busy and think it's a good place and so recommend it to others around there respective swimming pools during the day. So really I was redundant when Omar's was full, and it was every night, sometimes having to do two sittings to cater for all our customers. Our after-dinner entertainment needed a bit of livening up as our DJ Hasan, although enthusiastic, seemed to play music he liked himself (another trait of Turkish DJ's) and Hasan's particular love of country and western, in particular Kenny Rogers, wasn't creating the desired effect. In the end Hassan resigned himself to being the Cocktail maker and I took over as DJ when I figured the time was right. I was amazed to see that cheesy music worked a real treat with the Brits. One track got requested over and over and I found myself playing it every half an hour… Tarkan's 'kiss, kiss', a song I came to loathe. Playing it would see a mad rush onto the bar where girls of all ages would do the actions to this cheesiest of cheesy Turkish tracks that stayed in the Turkish charts for years!

Strangely, none of the waiters ever wanted to venture behind the bar until this track came on but a chance to see up the skirt of an unsuspecting holidaymaker was just too much of a temptation to resist! One particular night the bar staff were in for a shock though as a group of, let's say "plump", ladies from Blackpool just proved too much for the wooden bar and brought the whole thing down!

3

That Crazy Old Geordie

Intentionally or not, I don't know, but no-one told me I wasn't the only Brit working in our neighborhood. Although I had seen a grey-haired fella working across the road in a Newcastle shirt it was nothing new for the Turks to be given football shirts and I presumed he was Turkish until one of the customers mentioned to me one day that he was British and that was it. I went to investigate and there was this fella, in his fifties, from Whitley Bay, wearing a white shirt and dickie bow tie hassling tourists with his broad Geordie accent. Of course him being English meant he was getting people into his restaurant with little effort just as I was. After introducing myself I discovered he had arrived on the same day as me so God only knows how they kept us apart. Looking back you couldn't really blame them as later myself and Denny caused havoc for years to come. Without him this book just couldn't have been written. How the Turks looked on in amusement as from that day on we used to have our morning cuppa sat in the middle of the roundabout. We saw many Brits come and go, Denny and I, but we saw them all out. Eventually Denny would see me out as well as the old boy is still in Marmaris alive and kicking today. But whatever the reasons for any Brits wanting to work in Marmaris, I never did ask Denny what his was, it wasn't my business. I think he's only been home once since and for sure us meeting up made it a lot more enjoyable. Our

Turkish bosses would beg to differ though as at times we would lead them a merry dance. Sometimes we would finish work and go on benders in the afternoon. We were both skint but we knew how to play the Turks. We would promise them we would send customers to them. In the Turtle Bar in particular we would blag our beer all afternoon by me singing on the Karaoke and Denny explaining he was my manager and that I was a professional singer looking to work in Marmaris. We acted this scene out in just about every karaoke bar on the beach. After such benders and going straight to work at seven o'clock, I could plainly see Denny using his restaurant wall to prevent himself from falling over.

It was around this time that, without realising it, I discovered hassle in Turkey is strictly illegal. Although my boss had warned me a few times about going outside Omar's onto the pavement to try and coax them in, it never crossed my mind that the police would do under cover operations with cameras to try and catch hassle men whilst working. In so doing they caught restaurants out and they were closed down for six days. I wasn't aware of it at the time, my boss didn't want me to know, but his connections within the local police force meant we would always get a tip off when such an operation was underway. However, one night we didn't receive a tip off. Although I wasn't actually caught by the police, Marmaris TV were doing their own investigation into hassling and when they unexpectedly pointed a camera in my face, there I was in my hat full of cocktail umbrellas doing a dance for them. Little did I know the following day it was to be shown on Marmaris TV and I was quite a personality for a while.

However, without realising it, I was really getting the backs up of the local restaurant owners. Although the staff and I took great pleasure in seeing Omar's buzzing until two or three in the morning while our competitors had shut up shop and gone home, I was walking a fine line. There were many undercover police operations that season, fortunately my boss always seemed to know when. So on those particular nights I was to pose as a holidaymaker. Boy did I take advantage of the situation! Myself and Denny would welcome such nights although we dare not show it.

But it was getting that it wasn't Denny I needed, it was Yunus. It was becoming a weekly occurrence that Sevil would ring Omar's early in the morning and enquire who it was I was sat with the previous night as she had passed our restaurant and seen me sitting with some girls. Can I categorically state that, yes of course I used to sit and have a beer with customers after work and I had many chances, but I never once, at that time, slept with a tourist. But all too frequently she would tell me we were through and slam the phone down on me. Yunus smiled when I explained my dilemma as he knew only too well what Turkish women were like. "Paul it's all a game," he would insist. But I had seriously had enough of the accusations and sometimes would leave it two or three weeks before going down to Sevil's hotel on my afternoon break to make the peace. Or sometimes, out of the blue, Sevil would turn up at Omar's with her hotel guests. This always brought great pleasure to my boss who just saw dollar signs when her hotel guests would walk in.

Now as I've previously said, even up to today, I saw many crazy people come to Marmaris, so crazy and they knew it. However, one particular girl who walked in Omar's one day was a disaster and left a trail of destruction wherever she went. Her name was Sammy, a tall stunning blonde from Essex who came to Marmaris to be with her boyfriend James, real name Ajhan, from Diyarbakir. He was the manager at the Rosy Apartments just around the corner from Omar's. Sammy would often join Denny and I on our afternoon pub crawls and many a time we would all stagger home together. It was one such afternoon that she explained that her and James had split up and that I could move into the apartment with her if and when I wanted. Only a stone's throw away from Omar's it was perfect! My little top floor oven, although free of the cook now (he moved out because of my snoring), was really getting me down. Not only was it hot but the shower was forever without hot water and it seemed things had a habit of disappearing out of my room. I also had to run the gauntlet of Yelcin's mother when I stumbled home drunk at four in the morning. It was fortunate I didn't understand the Turkish names she would call me as I fell over her furniture in a bid to act sober and creep quietly past her. So here I was thinking lady luck had shone on me and together with Steven I carried my cases to Sammy's place. All settled in I went to work pleased as punch with my new living quarters.

Sammy was now a regular in Omar's and the boss would sit there all night staring at her ample boob job. One night after a long busy shift we walked the fifty meters to her apartment. In a drunken stupor after finishing a few bottles of wine on her balcony, we ended up in bed together. Suddenly it all went crazy. There was banging on the windows, people on the roof, hammering on the door and then finally someone trying to kick the door in.

"Paul, what shall we do?" asked Sammy, looking for an escape route. Jumping off the first floor balcony was not an option.

"There's nothing we can do!" I shouted.

"Just let them in," I said, hobbling with one foot in my jeans. It was obvious there was more than one person as the noise was just deafening from all over the apartment. Then it went silent for some reason and remained so for what seemed an eternity. After a while I peered out of the window into darkness. I checked the apartment over and decided to go back to Omar's to see if the lads knew anything. With the coast seemingly clear I slowly walked down the steps and down the dark pathway leading to Omar's and then I saw it, just a flash of silver as three lads jumped the fence. One, James, was armed with a cutthroat razor. As the other two proceeded to hold my arms out against the fence James held the razor to my throat and started to push his face filled with hatred into mine. "What the fuck you doing in my apartment with my girlfriend?" he screamed at me with an expression on his face that told me what ever I answered he was going to kill me! Knowing what I know now, him being Kurdish meant it would have not been a problem for him whatsoever. Now I don't particularly believe in God but somebody was clearly looking after me that night as even now I don't know how I managed it but I broke loose and ran to the lights of the main road and indeed the safety of Omar's where I prayed the boss and the staff would still be there because the sound behind me told me they were catching up fast. I'd made it and looking back down the pathway I saw my pursuers had disappeared. With a look of sheer terror on my face I was met by Steven who sat me down with the few late-night revelers left in Omar's. The music stopped and my boss came over and asked what had happened. When I finally got my breath back to tell him all hell broke loose. He instructed the staff to go to the kitchen and they came out with various weapons, Steven getting first choice of the meat cleaver which he tucked down his shorts and covered the handle by pulling his Rangers football shirt over it. "Paul who was it? Did you see them?" Steven enquired calmly. After I had explained it was Ajhan (James) we all went to the Rosey apartments. The lads walked around the grounds of the apartments looking for him while I stood with my boss at reception. The boss angrily quizzed the poor receptionist as to Ajhan's whereabouts. As we left he gave the ultimatum that if Ajhan wasn't sat in Omar's within fifteen minutes then we would be back. I heard later that Steven had been frantically strutting up and down the bar area shouting Ajhan's name and all sorts of Kurdish obscenities. He was surprised to see some Scottish customers of ours drinking in the Rosey's late bar. They got a bigger surprise when, taking a dislike to his Rangers shirt, they drunkenly tried to remove it only to discover he had this huge meat cleaver sticking up from under his shorts!

Sure enough by the time we got back to Omar's James was sat at a table with my boss, crying. I was hysterical.
"Come on you prick, just me and you now," I screamed at the top of my voice trying in earnest to scramble over the table to get to him.
"Paul I'm sorry. I'm drunk, I drink too much," he cried. After several more verbal outbursts the situation calmed down. When he later explained his side of the story I could understand his anger. He and Sammy had indeed split up but the apartment she allowed me to move into wasn't hers, it was his. He was paying for it. That night, not only did he see me move into his flat with his girlfriend, but also make out with her in his bed! Well the average Brit would have been pissed off never mind a fiery Kurd. Have no doubts about Kurdish people, they are a proud, proud race and to cross them you must be very brave, or very stupid. These people will die for their cause and that is a fact that even scares the living daylights out of the Turks.

The next morning, having spent the night back at my old place, I sat outside Omar's when Sammy walked in as right as rain as if nothing had happened. To say I was pissed off was an understatement and I let go a torrent of abuse mainly implying that she was indeed a fucking dumb Essex blonde! But Sammy being Sammy just took it all with a pinch of salt and headed off down the road with her cat, aptly named Raki, closely following behind her, tethered with a piece of string. I also had a visit from James that day. He brought me a sleeve of cigarettes. However, despite having made our peace, they never again recommended our restaurant to the guests stopping in the Rosy apartments. Unfortunately as it was the biggest and closest apartments to Omar's this was a big, big loss.

I have never forgotten that night and some years later, whilst on holiday in Marmaris with my wife and somewhat the worse for wear, I spotted James working in the Apache. With no ill intentions I went in and asked if he remembered me, he shook his head sheepishly and when I reminded him of his name and that he worked at the Rosy he claimed it wasn't him and that I must be mistaken. I never forget a face especially one that was going to cut my throat. Sammy and I made up and went on to nearly set the Hotel Seven on fire. But from that day on I promised myself never to get involved with British workers again and I never did. It seemed like the only time I used to see these girls is when they had problems with Turkish men. In all fairness they brought most of the problems on themselves by simply failing to educate themselves in the complexities of Turkish culture.

Denny and I got away with a lot simply because we knew the right people in the right places. Looking back at the whole incident that night, I think I had used up one of my lives. But it seemed I had a few more left and it is with this in mind it brings me to two brothers who, quite simply, were sent from above. I make no exaggeration in stating that without Mikail and Mehmet I would not be alive today and my memoirs would never have been penned.

Denny as Al Jolson

One of Denny's signs outside of Paradise restaurant.
"Bar shuts when last player falls over"!

Denny with the staff from Paradise Restaurant 1998

Denny as Tina Turner - those duck slippers became iconic

There are many pros and cons for a Brit to be working in Turkey. One of the cons, (my biggest ball ache) was that you get all the complaints from the customers, especially when I later worked at Bacchus, it used to drive me insane. The Turks make so many promises but fulfilling some of them is simply impossible and it always seemed to be me who had to pick up the pieces. I could point out many instances but on one such occasion my boss Mehmet at Omar's decided we were going to put haddock and chips on the menu. It was to be my job to recommend our great traditional British meal to our customers! Having explained to my boss that Cod and Haddock were cold water fish and that we simply couldn't buy it in the market he begged to differ and simply wouldn't listen to my reasoning. So without further ado off we went, on the back of his scooter, to Marmaris fish market. Oh yes there were many weird and wonderful sea creatures to be purchased but nothing that even resembled Haddock.

"This will do," said my boss as he handed over kilos of the fillets to be weighed. I looked on in disbelief. "It's Pollock Mehmet," I explained. "Pollock, Haddock, Cod it's all the same Paul," came his angry reply and I could see he was fast losing his temper. "Fish is fish," he went on. So off we went back to the restaurant where he had a sign all prepared for the launch of our Friday special. "Real Fish n Chips" read the florescent poster. What could I do? I was on a hiding to nothing and when people asked me "Is it like back home Paul?" What could I say? Consequently, that Friday was enough and after having what seemed like hundreds of disgruntled customers baying for my blood I simply slipped out of the restaurant, went down to Yunus's and got plastered! We never had fish on the menu again. On my return to Omar's for my nightshift my boss looked ten years older as I had left him to face the torrent of abuse. He never said anything about the incident but I was to have many such instances in the future. Indeed the cook and I would get to loggerheads about many a culinary disaster that came out of the kitchen. Especially the Turks love for filling plates with salad. Perfectly normal for their many dishes but on Sunday lunch and Curry? Bless them they try but try telling a chef what British people eat and you would think they had lived in the UK all their lives!

The biggest positive for a Brit working in Turkey, and it is a big one, is commission. Believe me all Turkish resorts are commission crazy. A small fortune can be made by resort workers. Let me explain. Jewellery, leather, clothing, Turkish baths, boat trips, car rental, in fact anything I used to recommend to my customers used to have something in it for me. Whether it be 20 percent off gold and leather or a free speedboat when I wanted it, I was always on a winner. I could quite simply recommend a nightclub such as bar X and I would be getting free drinks when I went in there. It's all "you scratch my back I'll scratch yours". So when our restaurant was full of Brits looking to purchase something it was always me they entrusted for a recommendation. All it took then was for me to scribble my name on one of our Omar Sharif cards and off they went believing that I was going to get them a discount because they were my friends and that as a Brit I knew all the places that could be trusted. So when you hear the Turks telling you his uncle, brother, cousin works at a jewellery shop for example, it's simply not true. They are just sending you to the shop which is going to give them the best commission and apart from a handshake at the start of the season they probably don't know these guys from Adam! If you are smart, as both myself and Denny were, you can, by the end of the season, make a small fortune. This method of making money is strictly forbidden by most Turkish bosses and understandably so. Having the ability at their disposal to make more money in one jewellery sale than you could make in a month as a resort worker means that some of the lads find themselves selling gold to their customers before they have given them the menu!

It was early on in my first season when a customer of ours asked me to recommend a gold shop and I innocently said I didn't know of any. Overhearing the conversation, our waiter Steven joined us and sneaked a business card across the table and assured them this was the best place in Marmaris. Having had my foot kicked under the table, I agreed. Like I said, although being strictly forbidden by the bosses, it goes on everywhere, is done by everyone and can lead to some heated arguments amongst restaurant staff. Only two years ago I found a couple who wanted to buy gold and took them to my restaurant for a drink first. For some reason I got distracted and was in my boss's office. On my return to the couple, the lads, having discovered they were about to buy gold, tried to muscle in on my prospective customers. I was fuming but that's how competitive it is.

Steven took me to a shop close to Omar's (the closer the better) and I was introduced to Mehmet (the owner) and Mikail his brother. After a lengthy discussion and a few free Rakis it was agreed that I would send my customers to their shop and receive a fifteen percent commission on gold and twenty percent on diamonds. They would also kit me out with an expensive bracelet on loan for the season to lure customers into asking where I obtained it. That day was not only the start to a very lucrative business between myself and the brothers but much, much more. They were like family for me and as you will find out later they saved my skin on numerous occasions.

A story in my first few months, that at the time just didn't make sense, became obviously apparent as I discovered this bonus. When I used to visit Sevil on a night at her hotel Jacob, the barman there, would inform all the hotel guests that his uncle would be arriving from Istanbul that night and that he was a jewellery dealer on a short holiday. Sure enough late on in the night his "uncle Ludwig" would arrive, sit at the bar briefcase in hand and proceed to supposedly get very drunk. Slowly but surely, as the families returned to the hotel and went to the bar for a nightcap. Dear old uncle Ludwig put his master plan into operation. With Jacob apologizing for his uncle's apparent drunken state he would introduce him to the guests. Far from sober themselves the guests were just falling over themselves to find out just what Ludwig had in his case. After much "persuasion" he would open the case to an audience that were astonished by its contents. Uncle Ludwig's case looked like some lost treasure from the Mary Rose! The masses of gold chains, rings, diamonds that stupendously shone from the case, lit up the eyes of the women. "Take them," cried Ludwig drunkenly, "take them all" and proceeded to fasten the gold chains around the necks of the unsuspecting British tourists. Having caused sheer chaos in the bar the wives and girlfriends found themselves going to bed with a four hundred pound chain around their necks. Despite the husbands' pleas to Ludwig for a price he would tell them he was drunk and they would talk in the morning. Job done. Ludwig knew the outcome and it worked every time. As the guests got up to their rooms and the wife admired her piece of bling in the room mirror, the husband, seeking to please his wife would, in a drunken state, promise his beloved she would not have to return the item. Sure enough the following morning Ludwig would be sat nursing his "hangover" with coffee and would know exactly who had taken the bait. The jewellery "borrowed" the previous night would sit there open to negotiations from the wives'/girlfriends' partners, eager to please. Worked every time. It seemed though "uncle Ludwig" actually lived in Marmaris. He used to pull the same stunt at a different hotel every night much to the delight of the staff as they shared out the huge pot of commission earned by their masterstroke! Ludwig is still around today and maybe you thought you had bagged yourself a bargain from the drunken old Turk, Ludwig, a real character.

Yes commission crazy Marmaris definitely was one of the perks of the job and a great way of subsidizing my income while I, and all the rest of the Marmaris workers, were waiting for their first payday from the bosses which could be as late as June/July. All the resort workers are in the same boat, getting money from your boss was not a weekly/monthly thing, he paid when he wanted something. I just couldn't comprehend and scary as he was, my boss at Omar's and I had fights over money on a weekly basis. But I learned the art of Turkish mind games from my mentor Yunus who was still giving me language and culture lessons. Sure enough after much "umming and arring" along with me threatening to leave the boss would eventually pay up. I had proved to be invaluable at Omar's and they couldn't do without me now. I had my boss by the balls and that's a massive advantage when it comes down to negotiations in Turkey. Indeed it is why so many Brits think they can work in Turkey. Sure they can, but unless you can prove your salt to the boss (and not many do) then you don't have a cat in hell's chance of getting paid.

Another means of making money is of course the tip box. The day myself and the cook opened the tip box I knew I had made it. I knew I was now the main man at Omar's. I had proved myself and the all-important job of counting the tip money was left to the two most important people in the restaurant, me and the cook. The tip box is a salvation to all the workers and is shared out on a pyramid structure. So if there was, for example, two hundred pounds in the tip box, myself and the chef would take fifty each and leave the rest to be divided out amongst the rest of the staff. This could mean as little as five pounds for the plate washer. This system works the same in every restaurant in every resort. Should you wish to work in Turkey and are to sit down and negotiate a salary then at the top of your negotiations list must be what is your percentage from the tip box. During peak season you would be surprised how quickly it is filled. Even when customers who, after their holiday finished, would slip twenty pounds in my hand I would always put it in the tip box. We worked hard together and we all had our part to play in keeping the restaurant going, it was only fair to share everything. In fact I remember suggesting to the cook once that we should share it equally. That was a suggestion that didn't go down well at all! Everyone has to work there way up the ladder in Turkey. I did used to feel sorry for some of the younger ones though s they desperately needed money to send home to their parents, but sentimentality and sympathy is something you have to learn not to give when working in Turkey. I found out in my first season, give your fellow workers a finger and they will take your arm. Never, as I did in my first season, show them weakness or for sure these young lads will walk all over you. I have heard many times from tourists that the head waiters and managers treat the waiters harshly and yes at times they do. But let me assure you when that same waiter one day climbs up that ladder to be a head waiter/manager himself he will treat his staff equally as badly. That's how it goes in Turkey, you must kick everyone's arse that is under you in order to gain their respect. Please, please don't feel sorry for them. Young Turkish waiters will exploit your weaknesses and in doing so lose all respect they may have had for you.

A few years ago, whilst walking through Armutalan, I came across a restaurant that I heard had been bought by an English man. Thinking I would pay him a visit and see how he was doing I was dumfounded to find him sweeping the floor of his own restaurant, as you probably would in England. His staff however were all playing on his newly acquired pool table. This poor bloke didn't last two minutes and neither will anyone who owns a restaurant and allows his staff one tiny piece of sentimentality!

We had an English barmaid working for us in the later years in Bacchus and her fellow bar staff would quite happily sit there and let her do all the work. One particular day I had seen enough and when one of them called her a bitch in Turkish I lost it and grabbed the boy by the ear schoolboy style and dragged him out of the bar. His Kurdish uncle, who also worked in the restaurant, came across asking what had happened. When I told him he took his nephew down the side of the restaurant and slapped him all over the place. As hard as it looks please understand that's the way it goes in Turkey. It's all about respect for your elders and your senior staff. "Abi" or "Bey" (big brother or sir) are all used by boys and men alike when addressing their elders or seniors. Respect, it's one of the things when living, working or buying a business in Turkey must seriously be addressed. It's a dog-eat-dog world in Turkey and the quicker you learn that the better.

4

To Greece and Back

Once a season truly begins in Turkey you simply lose track of time and dates. Quite simply you don't have time to think and, apart from Fridays, it doesn't even cross your mind what particular day it is. It must have been around my third month as I began to think about renewing my visa. As you are probably aware when entering Turkey and paying your ten pounds you are granted a three month Visa. This only gives you permission to stay in Turkey, nothing else. Working is strictly forbidden. Before your Visa runs out you must start making plans to leave the country for a day to get it renewed so giving you a further three months. These days it's no big deal but back then when very few Brits were in Marmaris it was pretty scary. Rhodes was the easiest option to obtain a fresh visa and could easily be done on the Hydrofoil. Using Marmaris harbour on your outbound journey was not a good idea as the harbour police always watched who was coming and going and asked a lot of questions. To make it less obvious people used to travel to other parts along the south coast and make the trip from there then come back through Marmaris. This was still a daunting experience though as the last thing you want is to be refused entry back into Turkey especially when all your belongings are there. After much deliberation it was decided I would sail from Fethiye, a one and a half hours drive from of Marmaris. The only problem was who would take me there as the drive would have to be done through the night in order to get catch the Fethiye/Rhodes hydrofoil at nine in the morning. On one particular night with my expiry date getting ever closer my boss informed me I would be leaving that night. So, having informed everyone I would be gone for a couple of days, I packed a small holdall and headed to Omar's for final instructions only to find out it had been cancelled and would now be the following night. That would be my final night in my little oven on the top floor. Yelcin's grandma was still screaming at me every night when I crept through her bedroom, things were still going missing from my room and the summer sun was making it impossible to breath in there never mind sleep. What happened that night was the final straw. Making the most of my night off I decided I was going to go down Bar Street with Yunus. On entering Greenhouse Nightclub and looking onto the dance floor for any familiar faces I couldn't believe what I saw! Thinking I was safely on my way to Fetihye, two of the lads who also lived in Yelcin's apartments, thought they would take the opportunity to borrow my belongings. They were dressed head to toe in my clothes! I was livid! When they saw me their faces were a picture but before the excuses could come out of their mouths they were about to feel my anger!! I made my opinion rather strongly felt, at this point they decided it was best to make a quick exit. As they hurried off a familiar odour was left in their trail, MY Calvin Klein aftershave! I informed my boss the next day and was assured he would find me somewhere else for when, indeed if, I got back.

That night saw me meeting up with the driver who was going to drive me to Fethiye. I can't remember much about the journey as I was half cut (as I was most nights then) and the guy couldn't speak a word of English. I did feel a little uneasy driving these strange roads in pitch darkness to a place I didn't even know existed with a complete stranger, but my boss had arranged it and that was good enough for me. Five in the morning and I was dropped off at Fetihye harbour wanting nothing more than a cup of tea. As I sat there on a bench overlooking the beach I was about to witness one of the most beautiful sunrises I had ever seen. Daylight broke through, Fethiye slowly revealed itself to me and what a breathtaking little resort greeted me that morning as I waited for the ticket office to open. A couple of hours later I was sat having a beer in Rhodes. I had visited Greece many times on holiday and loved the place however this time I wasn't on holiday and my intention was to get this over and done with and get back to Marmaris as soon as possible. So here I was arriving there in high season from Turkey and my main concern was just where would I sleep the night, everywhere was full. I got chatting with a Greek barman who had a friend of a friend who had rooms to let. With no more ado he called this guy who came on a scooter to pick me up and take me to my accommodation which, for only a tenner, was just what the doctor ordered. After a few drinks around the town I settled in for the night only for the constant screams of ecstasy coming from every room in the apartment to keep me awake. Yep you guessed it, my accommodations' main business was not from tourists but ladies of the night!

The next day I collected my ticket back to Marmaris and sat in the huge harbour at Rhodes awaiting my Seacat journey back. After a couple of hours baking in the morning sun I decided to enquire as to where the boat was. I had only been waiting at the wrong side of the harbour and missed it! Shit! Having informed the port of my mistake they realised I was alone, vulnerable and indeed living in Turkey. The Greeks fleeced me for nearly every penny I had but I eventually got a ticket for the following day and, having called my boss in Marmaris, who was far from happy, I found myself with plenty of time but little money and filled the rest of the day with a self guided tour of Rhodes. I must have walked around the castle walls what seemed like a million times.

"Life is like a box of chocolates, you never know what you're gonna get" was the famous quote from the film Forrest Gump and the same can be said about Turkish customs still today even though I have crossed the border many times I can't help but panic. It may be due to the film Midnight Express but you just never know what's going to happen when you approach passport control, these people are a law unto themselves. It can seem an eternity from when the grim-faced guard snatches your visa studies it and slams it back down on the counter. My return to Marmaris that morning was no different as he flicked through the pages of my passport. But having paid my visa I was free to go. Although I was to get many a grilling since and some very nerve-racking experiences especially at Dalaman airport, which for me, even with it's recently acquired facelift, remains a cesspit where laws don't exist and the people who work there see it as a last chance to fleece every penny from unexpecting holidaymakers. It doesn't stop at money, young ladies should avoid at all costs turning up drunk at Dalaman airport! The look of relief on my boss's face as I walked into the restaurant having evaded the many questions asked of me when re-entering Marmaris and obtaining the precious three month stamp. I felt like I had been gone a year as the lads in Omar's greeted me like a hero. All service stopped in the restaurant as I was mobbed by my colleagues while the puzzled customers looked on.

A few things had happened in my absence. Denny had left Prestige restaurant across the road and was now working a hundred yards down the street at Paradise restaurant. It also appeared I had a new apartment at the Star Hotel around the corner. I now had my visa and a new place to stay so I could relax and look forward to the rest of the season. For the next two months we were packed solid every night, we had our food and entertainment finely tuned now. The boss was happy, the lads were happy and as Sevil was going through one of her cold shoulder routines, I was also happy. I was not going to let anything stop the party and with me on top of my game it was time I let my hair down, as the saying goes "when in Rome…" For the last three months I had been pulling women into Omar's for the rest of the lads to enjoy. Now all that was about to change as it was my turn to party! The rest of the season would mean drinking a bottle of Vodka every night while working, going out until the early hours and sleeping with women of all ages and nationalities and after little or sometimes no sleep working all day in the unbearable high season heat, it was worth every minute… at the time.

Although I didn't see Denny that often I would sometimes pass his restaurant in the early mornings and creep into his living quarters at the back with a huge bucket of ice-cold water and throw the entire contents over him before making a hasty retreat as he would come screaming blue murder at me chasing me down the street in his boxers. He had his own gang down there though and one of them, Carlos, was a right card. Sadly, passed now from cancer, Carlos, who originated from Grimsby, had been in Marmaris years and had a car/scooter hire business across the road from Denny's place. His party piece was to sit behind his desk all day, drinking a bottle of Raki, and, unbeknown to his customers, stark bollock naked! Much to the amusement of all who knew, he would have the Turks in hysterics with his antics. Carlos, God bless his soul, was a huge bloke and as his partner Osman was later to find out, was not one to be messed with. The memory of him that sticks in my mind was when I had taken a rare visit down to see Denny one night and a group of us got wasted on Raki. Carlos decided we would go to his house in the mountains for a BBQ and a smoke of Turkish herbs. After inviting all the customers in Denny's restaurant, we had the dilemma of how would the dozen of us get to his house that was perched literally on the top of the mountain. After a long pause Carlos went to his shop and came back with a few sets of keys to his hire scooters and handed them out to everyone he trusted. Soon enough off we all went on our scooters, most of us with a customer sat on the back, up the long and winding road to his house. I don't remember getting back that night but I dare say it will certainly be in the memories of the holidaymakers who accompanied us that dark night.

It was at the Paradise restaurant that Denny started doing his "the worst belly dancer in Turkey routine" followed by his Rod Stewart, Tina Turner and Al Jolson impersonations. He still does them to this day. Although, may I say, not as enthusiastically. He could always pull in a restaurant full of customers eager to enjoy this crazy Geordie appear in a belly dancer's outfit complete with two of anything that fit into his bra, onions, oranges, socks, you name it. I have seen them fall out of it many a time. Yes, Denny was loving it down the street and his boss Tefik just let him get on with it. So seeing Denny pissed in those early days was nothing unusual, however seeing him absolutely obliterated was another thing especially when, in such a state one night, he decided to pay me a visit down at Omar's.

My boss loved Denny and couldn't do enough for him but this particular night he had simply gone too far as he walked in with Carlos and Osman and thought it would be funny to start winding our lads up by dancing with all the girls to everyone's amusement except our staff, who thought it was going to be their lucky night and my boss who was furious!

"Paul," he shouted beckoning me over. I leant down to listen to what he had to say over the music and his orders were quite clear.

"Throw fucking Denny out of my restaurant!" and he meant every word. In their wisdom Carlos and Osman had realised what mayhem they were causing and left leaving Denny clinging on to the table with the famous last words,
"Paul when this table stops spinning get me off the fucking thing will you bonny lad?"

Shortly after that night word spread that Denny had been arrested and was in Marmaris jail. Obviously his boss didn't have the connections mine had and some jealous Turk (we will come to who later) had called the police. As Denny had not been to Rhodes he was arrested because his Visa had expired. Obviously I couldn't go down to see him as it was far too dangerous but my boss went everyday. While Denny was in there, I committed an immortal sin! I drank a Geordie's Newcastle Brown Ale. Some customers of his had been in Paradise restaurant looking for him and hearing of his plight they were told to come and see me. They gave me four bottles of Brown Ale to look after until his release. Well, not knowing if or when he would be released, the temptation was all too much and I drank a couple of bottles. After a huge fine was paid and he was released Denny came in search of the said items and having admitted I had drunk half of his bounty he stormed off telling me to shove the other two bottles up my Yorkshire arse! Denny never talked to me for the rest of the season even though he had to pass me everyday on his suicidal ten mile morning jog to İçmeler he blatantly blanked me. I did get more bottles brought over and sent one of our waiters up to Paradise with them but they came back explaining,

"Paul, Denny not happy. He said put them in your arse sideways." Many times I held out my hand of friendship but the stubborn old git snubbed me.

Without my old chum I was content to spend the rest of the season causing chaos alone. Eventually the drinking, partying and sleepless nights began to take its toll and the whole "in your face" Turkish culture was beginning to wear me down. You see, what people experience when they holiday in Turkey is not real. What you see on the outside is mostly an act and once the music stops, the lights go out and the customers go home you see your colleagues in a totally different light. Under that smiling face, beneath that larger-than-life energetic Turk there is a rather childish, sad, almost pitiful person who seems to flourish in the spotlight and want to curl up and wallow in self pity in the shadows. No sooner had the guests left our restaurant off came the dance music they had eagerly strutted to all night and on came the tearful Turkish love songs. Most would sit and think of home and their families. Turks would call Kurds to me and how they brought shame upon Turkey. Kurds would tell of their persecution by the Turks. It was all rather depressing and tearful. Having heard the same old stories of woe for the last few months I would leave the lads to their melancholy Ibrahim Tatlises and head off to Bar Street with customers or Mico our head waiter. If I'm to be totally honest here, there is a hell of a lot of hidden resentment in every restaurant between Turks and Kurds and no matter how much the Turks tell me how free the Kurdish people were in Turkey (either they believed all they heard from the media or they simply knew the truth but wouldn't admit it) from where I stood, which was often between the two factions, the Kurds were persecuted. I know many a true Turkish national who would never consider talking to a Kurd apart from work related issues. For them it is simply unthought of. You may of course have been to Turkey and indeed not even know the difference between the Turks and the Kurds but if you want to find out what race they are simply ask a Kurd if he's Turkish and vice versa. The Kurdish people have their own language and indeed their own grammar, but up until recently with Turkey having to look at its human rights record in order to be given consideration for EEC membership, things were very different. The Kurdish people were strictly prohibited from speaking their own language to each other, playing Kurdish music, writing letters back home in Kurdish or purchasing music sung in Kurdish, from record shops. I'm no politician nor am I pro Kurdish or Turkish but I have listened to both sides of the story and I have seen with my own eyes what actually goes on. The Turks don't trust the Kurds and the Kurds don't trust the Turks. The Turkish call it the East of Turkey the Kurds call it Kurdistan. One thing is a well-known fact though, an estimated fourteen million Kurds live in Turkey and both the Turkish government and the Turkish people cannot underestimate the power these proud people have. Unemployment and poverty sees millions of young Kurdish men and boys travel the long distance to find work in Turkish resorts every season and quite simply, without these migrants, who are willing to turn their hand to anything to send money home to their villages, then Turkish resorts simply wouldn't find staff to enable their huge tourism machine to function. On the other side of the coin I can see the Turks point of view with regards to the current day problems these guys bring to resorts. However the problems lie much, much deeper and have done for a long long time. Indeed, as I write, the Turkish military are making daily incursions into the East of Turkey in an attempt to distinguish threats from the PKK but I can stipulate that from what I have seen and heard at first hand there are many other Kurds willing to take their place and give up their lives in an effort to claim back land that once belonged to them. I'm sure you can imagine what tension exists when Kurds and Turks have to work side by side on a daily basis.

As I've said before the Kurds are feared. Not only for their ability to hold Turkey to ransom with random and sometimes deadly bomb attacks but because they are fearless. Their lives which have been filled with torment and persecution means they fear nothing and nobody. Make no mistake you get into serious trouble with a Turk and your in for a hell of a fight, but fight with the Kurds and you are in serious, serious trouble as these guys will literally fight to the death.

The high season had left its mark on me in other ways too. I was a deep dark brown colour as keeping out of the daytime sun was not easy. There were times I felt the sun burning my face before quickly stepping back into the safety of the shadows. My hair was getting longer as I attempted to cover my neck with it but occasionally I would nip up the road to the barber and get a Turkish style trim, free of course, as everything was from the people who were on my recommendations list. After a quick shave off the sides I looked in the mirror and it dawned on me why people were now speaking to me in broken English. I was fast resembling a Turk. Speaking broken English to the lads in Omar's had become a habit that I couldn't shake off even when I was trying to coax tourists into our restaurant. Try as I might to prove to people I was English it wasn't easy. Not only to my fellow British holidaymakers but also to other Turks, especially the doormen on Bar Street who were convinced I was Turkish but spoke excellent English. As most of you are probably aware a Turk isn't allowed into bars and clubs without being accompanied by a lady and the reasons are pretty straight forward. They don't spend money, they hassle all the girls and they fight. Imagine my surprise one night when I went to Greenhouse with Hasan and after allowing him to take my date inside so he could gain access they refused me and left me angrily pacing up and down outside while Hasan and my date danced the night away! From that day on I used to carry my passport with me everywhere, particularly in Bar Street. As I often had problems getting in my boss arranged me a VIP pass for the big clubs down there. I actually was a frequent visitor to B52s on Bar Street and sent loads of customers to them as part of the bar crawl circuit. When I was refused entry one night I kicked off big time and the owner came to our restaurant the next day on his knees apologising because I had threatened to stop sending customers his way. I never had a problem in there again. A plus of my resemblance to a Turk was a game Yunus and I used to play. He would call me and ask me to come to his hotel as he had some girls sat at his hotel bar. I would play his Turkish cousin from Istanbul who spoke nor understood not one word of English. I would sit there in stitches as, when Yunus left the bar, the girls would quite openly sit there and talk about us thinking I didn't understand a word!

As I wrote earlier anything indeed is possible in Turkey and if I could write an entire chapter about the crazy things I saw that first season it would be endless. What most people would find bizarre, should they have witnessed it, I had grown immune to and it is quickly forgotten. However one particular story comes to mind that I just have to include. What started out as a bit of fun nearly caused a riot one Friday afternoon. Almost every street has a Turkish homeless alcoholic and ours used to roam the streets begging for money or beer. Now I've always been one for the underdog so, when the boss was not in the restaurant, I would always treat this man to a swift half on the understanding he would drink it and make a sharp exit. This day was no exception so, having quickly downed his beer, the vagrant went into the supermarket next door and Mehmet (yes another one), the owner of the shop would chase the beggar out with a brush after he would try and purchase a bottle of wine with his begging money. Having been ushered out of the shop and told in no uncertain terms he wasn't welcome, the vagrant proceeded to the middle of the roundabout outside our restaurant and started dancing to Tarkan's Kiss Kiss which could be heard blaring out from our music system. He was giving it his all, complete with all the actions. On seeing this, the hundreds of market goers who constantly streamed down the street stopped to take photos of him dressed only in denim shorts and sandles with a month's growth gracing his haggard face. Then I had a notion. I took full advantage of my three hundred and fifty watt sound system and went to full volume. By now he was in his element, Steven took a 100 lira out of his pocket, walked up to the roundabout and tossed it at the man's feet much to his joy. He was absolutely euphoric when the tourists followed suit and surrounded the roundabout taking photos and hurling masses of notes of all currencies at him! Only when the song had finished did he bend to his knees and begin to gather in his bounty, the amount, which I heard afterwards was some two hundred pounds, would see him live out the rest of the summer like a king. Hence we never saw him again but that sound system of ours would get us into serious trouble a few days later when the police closed Omar's down for three days.

It's not unusual to see an empty police car parked outside a restaurant in Turkey as the police like to stop in their own particular favourite restaurant for their free lunch. Restaurant owners feel obliged to cater for the local constabulary's every whim. Not much choice really as it's always better to have them on your side. A free lunch now and again is a small price to pay for a nod and a wink should anything big be going down. However one night while our boss was away I saw just what can happen should you cross the local police force.

In those early days music was allowed until 2am but if you didn't take the mickey, you could go on through the night if you had contacts in the right places. Sure enough, come the deadline out came the police with lights flashing. Every restaurant was told to turn their music down or indeed off. Me, being the DJ, knew instinctively that out of respect, as soon as the police car drew up then down went the volume. Depending on the mood of the boys in blue I could either turn it back up or in most cases call it a night. The third option was to wait until they had gone and raise the volume again but it was my boss who made those decisions and I always waited for the nod from Mehmet before resuming the party. However this particular night he wasn't there and he had entrusted Omar Sharif (his brother who was on holiday from England) to keep an eye on things. Unfortunately it all went wrong as he foolishly rubbed the police officers up the wrong way with his English mentality. People seem to think that Turks are Turks and that wherever in the world they reside they all understand each other's thinking. That's a foolish mistake to make. I will embark on this later but for now I will just say that Turks who have lived in Europe for a long time just do not understand how things work in Turkey anymore. Although they might speak the same language in some cases this is as close as they get. To start preaching to the police about how we do things in Europe might sound impressive, but the Turkish police are not in Europe and still do things Turkish style which, like it or lump it, is "end of story". So when I saw Omar go over to speak to the police and getting into a heated discussion with them I just knew there were going to be consequences, and there were. A few days later our boss lined all the staff up and explained that due to us not complying with the police we were to be closed down for three days. The boss was clearly devastated by the thought of three days loss of takings when he explained we had three days off. We all listened looking suitably mournful. As soon as the boss's. back was turned though we were all excitedly making plans for what we were going to do on our three day vacation.

Getting closed down for three days doesn't sound that much of a disaster but believe me it is. Especially for us being full every night, it gave our competition a chance to steal our regulars and spread malicious gossip as to why we had in fact been closed down. It's so easy for other restaurants to start rumours that we had been closed down for hygiene reasons and the word soon gets spread through Chinese whispers. So when myself and Hasan decided we would hire a car and take three days holiday my boss had other ideas. He wanted me to stay outside hassling but obviously not to gain customers but to explain the reasons why we had been shut down. I was gutted and after some negotiation with him I made some huge fluorescent posters explaining that we had indeed been closed down for our music then I was allowed my three days holiday. What a sad sorry sight Omar Sharif's restaurant looked all sealed off in red and white tape. As Hasan and I passed on our way to Turunç that morning we had a split-second feeling of remorse, then we were on our way. It was to be a day when I was to use up another one of my lives.

We behaved like holidaymakers. Hasan and I did all the usual tourism trails, village tour, waterfalls and even a few bars before heading off back to Marmaris. As we headed up the mountains a black cloud opened up and we were hit by a thirty second torrential downpour. Having driven though the worst of it and proceeded down the steep decline, I was admiring the beautiful view over the cliff on our right-hand side when we hit a slippery patch in the road. We went into a terrifying spin! I only remember watching Hasan calmly fighting with the wheel to avoid the hundred foot drop as we span uncontrollably. We finally came to a stop only inches from the cliff edge. I can safely say that anyone other than Hasan at the wheel and we would have been killed. Even after all these years Hasan still reminds me just how good a driver he is and I am in total agreement! It was later when Hasan was bragging about his exploits to our boss's friend, Birol, that he got a severe telling off. It is a well-known fact that driving on roads after rain in Turkey is extremely dangerous. This is because the diesel, left behind by thousands of vehicles, had dried up in months of summer sun and it resurfaces once the rain falls and turns roads into ice rinks!

Our three day holiday quickly passed and it was back to business. However I had another dilemma. I had been thrown out of my third hotel as my boss hadn't paid my bills. So once again I found myself angry and homeless, only this time I had serious intentions of going back home as I was sick to death of being passed from pillar to post! Once again, with the promise that this would be a permanent move, I was moved to the top floor of a Dutch hotel directly opposite Omar's. Surprisingly it was like a penthouse and perfect apart from the disadvantage of being so close to Omar's so I was easily obtainable should things go wrong and I was needed in the restaurant. My new apartment was the envy of all the lads who I worked with and would remain my home for the remaining three months of the season.

My situation with Sevil was beginning to get intolerable and although I was getting advice from Yunus with regards to my relationship with a Turkish woman, things were not good. The sheer complexity of our culture clash was really getting to me and the frustration of seeing Turkish men openly flirting with European girls and bragging about it while I had to make do with a few stolen kisses once in a while was driving me insane. Yes we did get a couple of days off together but we couldn't walk on the same side of the road in case we were seen and it was only on the few occasions when time off meant we could take the bus leave Marmaris and reach the relative safety of Datça that we could be ourselves. It was these such times when we would sit and talk about the future but the more we talked the more I learned what an uphill battle this was going to be. In the meantime she would go back to Istanbul and stay with her family. If they ever learned of her relationship with me they would disown her. If she came back to England with me I would have to obtain a Visa for her and find work in England to support us both. The trouble was how could I find work when I would have to be her full-time babysitter as she would have inevitably struggled to adjust to English life. So what was the solution? Well I could convert to Islam, believe me there were many times I contemplated it. But I'm not a hypocrite. I have never been a religious person so why would I convert to another religion when I don't believe in God, any God. Plus the fact that my fear of hospitals and injections meant circumcision just wasn't an option!

We were stuck in limbo. While seeing her nearly every day was great, I wanted her to myself and this simply wasn't going to happen. I just couldn't see any light at the end of this long complex tunnel. Although you read of these relationships in fairytales I was a realist and was slowly beginning to realise that we were going nowhere. Through no fault of hers or mine over the next few months we would simply drift apart knowing that we had so much love for each other but unfortunately love was not enough. Sadly this fairytale although not quite finished, wouldn't have a 'lived happily ever after' ending.

I was still playing the field and my new apartment was the ideal love nest. The only problem I had was that the hotel owner used to actually charge me three British pounds should a lady stay with me for the night. It became a game of cat and mouse as I tried to avoid the added costs by sneaking ladies in late when I thought no-one was looking. I actually told ladies to leave by themselves in the morning in a bid to make the hotel staff believe it was just a hotel guest. Unfortunately the bastard always had a smile on his face when he caught me out and would hold out his hand in a morning for payment. I still don't know to this day how he used to know when I had someone stay with me but it was extremely rare I would escape the payment.

That apartment saw the best out of me when it came to women and one lady, Fiona from Chester who came on holiday with three friends actually stayed in my room for her entire fortnights holiday. She only left the room to get vodka and cigarettes. I was to learn something while in that apartment that would stick with me until this day. Now I'm not religious nor am I superstitious but something happened while I was in that apartment and it all started like this. There were times when I slept with ladies and maybe got a couple of hours sleep if any. Without fail I had to be at Omar's by nine o'clock for breakfast service. You can imagine there were times when I simply didn't have time to shower as it would always be a mad dash to make it for work. Although I knew I was breaking a strict law of Islam, to me it didn't matter. I was a Christian but it was brought to my attention one morning that indeed Christian or not it was important for me to shower as I was genebet. What is genebet? Okay the first I heard about it was when the boss's brother came to Marmaris for a holiday. Omar was a strict Muslim and one particular morning I saw him pacing up and down outside our restaurant. He called me over. "Paul, please can I have your apartment key, please I need to use your shower I'm genebet." So without thinking about it I handed him my room key and thought no more of it until he came back fifteen minutes later. He handed me my keys and I asked him "What does it mean, genebet?" He went on to explain that all Muslims must shower after sex, which I knew already, but if you don't shower you are genebet and superstition has it that you will be unlucky and that bad things will happen to you. Therefore he never came into the restaurant that morning because he felt if he did it would curse the restaurant.

"What a load of old tosh," I thought as I took my keys from him. I was to learn that there is a lot of truth in this superstition as sometimes our restaurant would, for no obvious reason whatsoever, be totally empty in a morning.

These mornings coincided with the days I didn't take a shower. From that day on I religiously took a shower in the morning even if I was late and we never had a problem again. If you ask a Muslim what it means to be genebet he will probably smile because it's superstition but for me it is one that I honestly believe.

Omar's quickly recovered from our closure and just when our competition thought we were finished we dealt our ace in the form of Karaoke. Although other restaurants had it, they didn't have an Englishman who, although I say it myself, was not a bad singer and could definitely create the right atmosphere. Once again Omar's found fresh legs and our after-dinner entertainment became so popular we had to use empty beer barrels as tables as customers reserved a table before they had even eaten such was our reputation. I also took great accolades for being the first to bring the Full Monty to Marmaris. It involved our waiters stripping off suggestively on the bar. We had been warned on several occasions that this could mean another closure but we had police spotters on every street. On a few occasions our show was abruptly ended mid thrust as our spotters gave us the signal that the police were approaching. A huge club in İçmeler tried to copy our stunt but got caught and they were actually closed down for ten days as well as having their good name splattered all over the local newspapers. Ironically that club were to offer me a job the following week and although I wasn't particularly bothered about a move I was eager to find out how much I was actually worth.

I decided I would borrow a scooter from Carlos and head up to talk with them. Just as I approached the Negros after the roundabout I was pulled over by the police. Although I protested my innocence and told them I was merely a holidaymaker they took me across the road to the police station and there I was held and my fingerprints were taken. My first real brush with the law saw me sat in the police station in a state of panic and when the door opened and they called me in for the interview how pleased was I that the police officer was a regular in Omar's. As we proceeded through the rigmarole of having my fingerprints taken he actually reached in his bottom drawer "Pol Raki istiyor musun?" he smiled asking me in Turkish if I wanted a glass of Raki. So we sat there, him talking Turkish and me nodding in agreement but not being able to comprehend a word he was saying. My boss Mehmet soon arrived smiling and after a brief discussion with the desk sergeant I was allowed to leave. I understand it cost my boss a fair bit of money as they had intended to close Carlos and his car hire business down because he lent me the scooter without insurance. But I was beginning to get touted by other restaurants, something my boss was well aware of and he I knew I had him by the balls. He couldn't afford to lose me and although I had never given leaving a second thought, mind games are a very powerful tool in Turkey. I was holding my cards close to my chest but occasionally just letting my boss know I was now holding a very strong hand.

You know if ever there was a finer example of the phrase "ignorance is bliss" then I would recommend the saying to anyone going on holiday to Turkey to see it, feel it, enjoy it but never dig deeper because it can literally change your whole idea of Turkey. I will point out what you see in these resorts isn't the real Turkey, far from it. You know it's crazy, you would think the more you understand a culture the easier it would get. However this definitely is not the case in Turkey. It gets harder, much, much harder and I found myself later realising just how tolerant the Turks were with tourists. I actually started to look at English people through Turkish eyes and if I'm honest I was often ashamed of my own nationality. But on the same level, our free-spirited British nature allowed the Turks to see a situation and take full advantage and some of their antics made my skin crawl.

One particular incident comes to mind that first summer. Now I, of all people, know the dangers of Raki and believe me I have witnessed at first hand what it can do to a man. Although I'm not proud to admit it I have drunk enough of it to know what to expect from this demon drink. I always respected it and that's where many a holidaymaker make a huge mistake. This drink is the devil in disguise and of all the holidaymakers that came and went it was the loudmouths who disrespected Raki and paid the price. That gave me a giggle but this particular fella who was sat at the bar with his wife and teenage daughter played with fire and got his fingers burned. I'm sorry to say he did deserve the consequences of not respecting the drink but didn't deserve what was about to unfold. "Raki, give me another Raki," he asked. It was the norm for me to oversee the customers and I politely informed the fella on the perils of a session with Raki. I told him to take it easy as he had gone through half a bottle. He proudly told me that he could handle his drink and that he wasn't even feeling any effects of the six or seven glasses he had already consumed. So, against my advice, he continued and knowing that it was only a matter of time before it took effect, I took a backseat and let the fuse wire burn. Thirty minutes later the big man with the big mouth who could handle his drink was transformed into a quivering wreck. As usual it was up to me to pick up the pieces without making too much of a commotion so as not to disturb our other guests. Now this guy was twice my weight but somehow I managed to get him up and, closely followed by his wife and daughter, I struggled with him the five hundred yards back to his hotel. Finally making the flight of stairs to the first floor I released him and he collapsed onto the bed. Turning to his wife to wish them goodnight, I found I was talking to myself. They had vanished and it wasn't rocket science to know where they had vanished to. I had seen the attractive mother getting attention from Mico so was becoming to think maybe this scenario had been set up as Raki is a particular favorite tonic for Turks to use when they wanted to get rid of someone. Getting back to the restaurant my suspicions were confirmed as the mother was now in slow dance mode with Mico and little September was happily embracing the daughter. Right over my head it went as I bid the lads goodnight and headed off to Bar Street. The following morning I arrived at Omar's for breakfast service only to find us two waiters down and as I sat down for my early morning cuppa the lads seemed sheepish. When I enquired what happened after I had left the night before I was told that our waiters had taken the mother and daughter to the Sun Hotel (tenner a night apartment come whorehouse). With disbelief I looked up and saw the four of them coming up the road holding hands! I later found out they had booked rooms next to each other and while the mother and Mico enjoyed a night of passion with Mico so did her daughter with September only a few feet away. The husband and father laid nursing a huge hangover and probably feeling the effects of a virgin raki drinker. We never saw the family again but I was to see incidents like this for the next ten years. As I've said you get immune to anything and everything. There were only a few occasions later on that made me raise my eyebrows and think 'this is fucking crazy'! Everything is crazy in Marmaris and it helps to get crazy as well because if you don't and you want to make everything an issue then for sure it's going to fry your brains!

Apart from customers there was another very important person that was welcomed with open arms even though he never spent a penny in our restaurant… the postman! When we saw him we were like kids at Christmas and we would all sit there hoping he wasn't going to pass us by leaving us empty handed. When he walked in he was greeted like the Messiah and once we had sat him down and offered him food and drink he would reach into his sack and hand over a handful of letters. They would be distributed to all and we would go off to find our own space to read our letters in secret. Well I say secret but I would get to read most of the letters as I was our restaurants' English translator. On these days I was the most popular guy in Omar's and it brightened up my day as well because some of the letters I translated for the boys from ladies had me in stitches. If only they knew! I would receive letters from home, friends, family and girls. The most unusual presents I received through the mail were knickers sent from girls. The best present I ever received was a cassette tape from my two kids Corina and Paul and as I sat on my bed listening to it I cried rivers. Of course sometimes it would be weeks before we ever saw the postman and on these occasions we would go down to the bazaar and ask for the mail at the post office. They would handover a huge bundle dating back weeks, the postman just didn't have time to deliver all the mail in the height of summer so it sat there gathering dust.

Only one person didn't really want to see the postman…our poor boss Mehmet. We would all sit there reading our mail and smiling but Mehmet would sit behind the cashier desk swearing and cursing as he read through his pile of final demands for gas, water and various other bills which went straight in the bin. Mehmet, as with most Turkish bosses, didn't want to pay for anything. I know we Brits are not particularly happy when we get bills and we moan and groan before paying them but the Turks simply ignore them.

Nothing, and I mean nothing, gets paid until people come knocking for money and then the money owed enters a new phase. They will sit down over tea and discuss the debt and decide that they will pay a sum now and then some more later and both go away happy until later never comes. Then the same guy comes knocking again and the same thing happens and it goes on and on. I remember our restaurant buying a new amplifier for our Karaoke. Mehmet and I went down to the music shop in the centre and I sat in the shop trying out various pieces of equipment. When I decided on one in particular Mehmet sat down with the shop owner to talk about the price. We were there for hours! Now both you and I would give the shopkeeper the money and be on our way but that's not the Turkish way. The Turkish system means that you pay a little and the shopkeeper will visit you a thousand times throughout the season for a payment and a free beverage that's how Turkish business works. The taxman doesn't send you a bill he just turns up at your establishment and takes everything out of the till. Indeed on such days if you are lucky enough to get a tip off that the taxman is in the area then you make sure you have no more than twenty lira in your till at any one given time! For those that are accustomed to Turkish business practices then you will be reading this with a smile on your face. The same goes with a Turk who wants to buy a pair of shoes. You or I would go to a shoe shop, see some shoes we like, try them on and if we liked the fit we would pay the shopkeeper and go home happy. But oh no, not the Turks, as I found out first hand when Hassan asked me that first season if I would like to come to the bazaar with him as he wanted buy some shoes.

Now for those of you who think it's a pain in the arse taking your mother shopping then think again. Although Hasan was only spending around a tenner we visited every shoe shop in the bazaar that long week. He would go to one shop, try a pair of shoes on, parade in front of the mirror then tell the shopkeeper he'd think about it. This would go on for days in different shops each day until eventually he bought the shoes he tried on first! What amazed me was that the shopkeepers weren't bothered by this behaviour at all…it was the norm. I on the other hand had had my fill of looking, trying on, negotiating, drinking endless tea before finally leaving the shop without a purchase, I was near to suicide! I never went shopping with Hasan again. Steven was sometimes sent to the Friday market to buy fruit and veg for the restaurant, for you and I this would be a twenty minute trip to Tesco. To a Turk it turns out to be a full day as each fruit is squeezed and tested before negotiation. Turks carry this trait with them when in Europe. When I was in Holland nothing infuriated the Dutch market traders more than seeing their nicely stacked oranges being totally wrecked by a Turk looking for a fruit that met their approval.

Lots and lots of spare time together with endless glasses of tea makes negotiation a pastime in Turkey. Another example is when two cars have a bump, both drivers come out shouting and screaming at each other and it looks like it's going to turn nasty then, from nowhere, someone brings a tray of tea out and like some miracle cure the tea calms them down they look at each others cars, decide who was at fault, sit down some more and drink more tea, hand over some cash and shake hands, job done!!

Both the cold nights and the diminishing amount of holidaymakers coaches coming into Marmaris told me it was getting very late on into the season and as much as I didn't want the season to end the truth is I was running on empty. The season had taken it's toll on me and the sun, drink, long days and even longer nights had left their mark. As much as my head was still willing I'm afraid my body wasn't. I was also not eating correctly and sometimes not thinking clearly. That last month saw me lose my temper with colleagues on a few occasions. I walked out numerous times only for the boss to send someone around to my room to coax me back. Yes I was well and truly burnt out and I suppose it was a relief when my boss came and sat next to me late one night and told me I would be going home the following week and after laying four hundred pounds on the table he told me to take a few days holiday.

The end of the season is always a sad time as you leave behind your workmates and friends. Just as we all arrived in Marmaris from all over so we were now leaving to go home to our respective cities. I have come to appreciate it's a time when saying goodbye to friends you have worked, lived, eaten and breathed with for six months could be a last goodbye. Over the years I have lost touch with people who were very close to me. The army, university or jobs in their own cities mean that a season in Marmaris is no longer possible. So each kiss and handshake could be your last. You do grow close and your restaurant team are more like family. I always felt vulnerable when I didn't have them around me. As for Sevil I never did say goodbye. As far as I was concerned it was over and after sending a huge bunch of flowers to her hotel I proceeded to pack my bags and waited for Hasan to take me to Dalaman. It was time to go and saying goodbye to my friends and colleagues there were many tears. I wasn't even out of Marmaris yet and I was missing the boys already.

When I got to Dalaman I began to think realistically about my return home, something I hadn't thought about for six months. In three hours I would be landing in Manchester to friends family and ghosts, lots of them. I also had to think of my finances because the fact that I hadn't saved a penny for winter meant I would have to get a job immediately on my return to the UK. What I should have done was lived Turkish style and saved for winter during that summer but I didn't. That would definitely be my last summer as a spendthrift worker. I had learned my lesson and cursed myself as I counted my seasons earnings. Although my return flight was paid for by my boss I had had to pay off the credit I had built up in various shops so I was left with about one hundred and fifty pounds to last me through the English winter. I kicked myself because I could have easily saved a couple of thousand pounds.

It was strange to be back home if I could call it home now. From the moment I landed in Manchester I was counting the days to the next summer. Karl, my best friend, picked me up and the atmosphere in the car was solemn as I replayed the season through my head as we hurtled along the M62. As we went under the Humber Bridge and into Hull itself I realised this was not my home or country and I didn't want to be here. Turkey was my home and even as I write this book thirteen years later I still consider it my home.

I don't want to bother you with the tedious stories of my return home as nothing much happened that winter. It probably did, but compared to Turkey it was childsplay and after moving into my friend's house and getting a part time job in Karl's pub it was just a case of hibernating and waiting for summer.
Christmas and New year came and went. I had booked a twelve week Turkish language course in Hull. Despite having had a season under my belt and a reasonable grasp of the Turkish Language, I felt this course would help me. I'm afraid to say it was a waste of time as what they were trying to teach us was proper Turkish and Turkish spoken in its correct form is just not spoken in holiday resorts. I often called the lads and my boss to see how they were and in general was trying to keep my head down. Thankfully that long winter back in the UK was about to get shorter, I received a telephone call out of the blue from Mehmet informing me that Hasan had been called into the army and Mehmet needed me in Marmaris in March as we would be renovating Omar's.

So, having once again said my goodbyes to friends and family, I was on the minibus on my way to Manchester airport. Unlike last year I wouldn't be going out there on the off chance not knowing what to expect. This year my flight ticket had been paid for. I would be living at my boss's house and in Hasan's absence I was the new manager of Omar Sharif restaurant. If I thought last year was a ball then this season was going to be even better! Winter had given me a lot of time to think and of course I wanted the good times that a Marmaris summer can bring but this year I had responsibility's, this year I wanted to be taken seriously, this year I didn't have to prove myself to others but I wanted to prove myself to me. This season it would be me making the decisions and those decisions would ultimately mean earning money not only for my boss and for myself but our staff and their families, this year would be a different type of challenge and I rose to it so much so that it ended in a way that I could never have imagined, read on.

With maybe fifty quid in my pocket I touched down at Dalaman that sunny morning in March and I was determined I was going to survive on my earnings and still save. Not that I had to of course but more that I wanted to. When my boss and his friend picked me up it was explained what was expected of me that summer, starting with the renovation of Omar Sharif Bar and Restaurant.

It seemed strange waking up in my boss's house in Marmaris. Me in one bed and October (one if the twins) in the other. That morning Mehmet and I walked down to Omar's so he could show me what we would be doing to the place. It seemed strange seeing the restaurant all boarded up. As much as I tried I couldn't imagine the great times we had in there. It seemed so small, as the boss unlocked the door I wanted to cry for the place. I was eager to have the doors opened, the cobwebs blown off and to bring the place back to life. After a quick summary my boss handed me the keys to both the restaurant and to his house. Before I had the chance to ask him why he was wearing a suit and tie he informed me he had gone into politics over the winter and was running for election. I would attend many meetings with him in the coming weeks. Although I wouldn't call them meetings really just BBQs and Raki with people in very high places. Mehmet amused them with tales of all my mistakes the previous summer. One in particular was when what I considered to be a nice piece of hardboard I could write a menu on, turned out to be his father's praying board that he used to kneel on during his prayers! Needless to say he wasn't very happy when he found it tied to the lamp post with "FULL ENGLISH BREAKFAST" written all over it. Another thing my boss taught me at those BBQs is that when eating fish then you must drink Raki or the fish would cry! Wow, I thought, what a great excuse as I poured myself another glass from the endless supply of Raki that adorned the table.

So after handing me the keys my boss went on his way and after a brief pause and a heavy sigh I closed the door to the restaurant and decided I would go for a walk. Having walked no further then fifty yards I saw a distant figure walking towards me with a wheelbarrow, as the figure got closer I vaguely recognized someone who could have easily been mistaken for a vagrant… Denny. The fact that he had stayed in Marmaris through the winter meant I was probably the first English person he had seen for six months and the previous seasons' fall out was quickly forgotten as he dropped everything and give me a big hug like some long lost friend. "Fancy a pint Den," I asked and before I knew it he was dressed shaven and looked more like summer Denny again. As we headed to the beach looking for a watering hole, so my intentions of living Turkish style and saving my money quickly went down the drain. Denny began to tell me of his first winter's stay in Marmaris. So we made up and as we had two months until the start of the season surely we could cause some mischief. Again read on.

Staying at my boss's house was not ideal at all. For one reason, I had September praying all bloody night in the bed next to me. Secondly I think the twins resented me being there and they would often both make my life hell, the reason being, I think, was that they thought I was treading on their toes. Mehmet trusted me and they didn't like that one bit. All the twins thought about was their family in Izmir and getting as much money to them as possible. As you read on you will see they would steal from their brother and from the restaurant to send back to their family. They resented Mehmet as they thought the money he was making on the restaurant he was gambling away down the Bazaar playing backgammon. As much as gambling is strictly forbidden so is stealing and the twins were not only stealing from their brother but from the restaurant as well, meaning they were stealing from all of us. They thought me being there would put an end to their devious ways. They asked me daily, "Paul what you doing here in Turkey, why you not fuck off back to England?" At first I took it all with a pinch of salt but these two made my life hell at Mehmet's house and I stayed away as much as possible, either at Denny's little room at the back of the Paradise Restaurant or, later, at Yunis's flat in the Bazaar.

My friend Yunis was now working at the Yapi Kredit bank on the marina and he carried me through until summer as I would often meet him after work and he would pay for supper and the odd night out in

Greenhouse. My days were spent with Denny. As we were both skint we needed to formulate a plan and we decided to hire ourselves out to the highest bidder for building work, our price being?… the price of a bottle of Raki! So after a hard days graft we would stop off to buy our Raki and a dozen eggs and have a Raki or six and boiled egg butty feast at Denny's. This went on for a good few weeks until we came up with another plan. Why don't we open Omar Sharif's early for Turkish customers to come and watch football on Cine Beş (channel five). So after having ploughed the rest of my money into the venture, the following day found us marching up to the Efes Beer factory to buy two crates of Efes at wholesale price on which we planned to make a healthy profit.

After giving the restaurant a good cleaning we opened. Denny and I doing the service and about twenty members of the Marmaris police force as our regulars. What's more we were making a nice little earner from them, we also often had the cheek to tell them that if they didn't like our prices they could go somewhere else! How's that for impudence?! When Mehmet came in we also sold my boss beer at our prices and it was his bloody restaurant!

After lengthy discussions on what we should do with the restaurant Mehmet assured me that work would begin soon. Little did I know it was me and Denny who would be doing most of it! I remember spending my April birthday sat on a pile of bricks in the restaurant with a case of beer and a few friends (the reps were beginning to arrive) listening to the restaurants entire music collection "Now that's what I call music 43". The following week

Denny and myself were summoned to the restaurant by Mehmet to make plans. Mehmet being Mehmet these plans were, let's say a little unconventional. So in broken English he explained that the Belediye (local council) wouldn't give him planning permission to extend the restaurant but he was going to do it anyway. It had to be done under the cover of darkness though. So that night Denny and I would begin to extend the perimeter wall of Omar sheriff by three foot all the way around and when we enquired as to where we would get the sand and cement from "there" he pointed to the restaurant across the road who had, just that day, had a lorry load of sand delivered. So as we arrived that night and Mehmet explained to us that the job must be done before sunrise the following day he beckoned me over. "Paul there is a bottle of Raki in the kitchen for you both but please, please don't open it until the job is finished," and off he went. An hour later and we were quite happily wheelbarrowing sand and cement across the road already having consumed half the bottle, one bottle led to another and we were making good progress, or so we thought, by six in the morning and well into our second bottle the job was finished. Off we went for a well-earned kip at Denny's gaff.

Denny and I lived on egg butties in those days and having devoured our second for breakfast we decided to go to Omar's to inspect our handywork. However one look up the road told us our work had been far from handy as my boss could be seen in the distance kicking down our wall while screaming all sorts of obscenities. We quickly decided we would take a detour and give him time to cool down. Having walked around the block we were relieved to see he had long gone but the remains of our brickwork was being cleared up by the twins. On close inspection you could see the reason for his anger, the wall started well but after a few meters… and rakis… it all went downhill. Well downhill, uphill, left, right, anything other than straight as the Raki's effects sapped our enthusiasm and judgement. From that day on Mehmet never asked us to do anymore building work in the restaurant and thus we had to concentrate on our nighttime Cine Beş customers to finance our drinking habits.

Some days later Denny and I had been given some work on the Market next to Omar's. This particular day was a huge day for my boss as election day had finally come round. How proud he was that morning admiring himself in the mirror before he left the apartment to join his fellow politicians as they set out to win the minds of last-minute voters. He took his place in the huge entourage of vehicles which was about to circle Marmaris. If you have never seen an election day in Marmaris then it's a sight to treasure. At the front of the parade are the Mercedes and BMWs of the three big parties and inside sat smartly dressed businessmen adorned with their party colours smiling and waving at onlookers while the professional sounding PA system fitted to the roof of their election bus urged you to vote for them. Then behind the three main parties' vehicles the forms of transport deteriorated. In the middle of the procession were the lesser-known parties in their white rental cars and Ford Cortinas (Taurus). Their politicians going for the jeans and smart shirt look. Then after the mile long parade of tooting horns and pleasant 'vote for us' type messages you would find the tailenders and the radical parties driving anything from battered out circa 1970 Russian rust buckets to tractors and scooters and their messages were screamed at you. "Vote for us or we will torture your family!" Okay slight exaggeration but judging by their dress and body language I think I could easily be persuaded to put a tick for them in my ballot paper! So round and round they went for hours and up their amongst the front end sat my boss in one of the lead cars in his suit and huge yellow rosette, smiling and waving to bystanders and trying to ignore me and Denny who were looking on in hysterics. Then an idea came to us although we knew it would not impress Mehmet. We decided we would join his party on the next lap so got ourselves prepared! As they came around again for what must have been the tenth time that afternoon my boss looked on with disgust as behind his election car was a wheelbarrow with me pushing it and Denny inside letting out a huge hooray as he tossed huge amount of yellow confetti style paper into the air! The onlookers found it rather funny but the look on Mehmet's face told me I better stay at Denny's for a couple of nights!

Truth of it all Denny and I were getting bored and I suppose it was a bit like the last of the summer wine as we tried to find mischief to relieve our boredom. We didn't have to look too far. I couldn't hack sleeping at Mehmet's, the twins drove me crazy and the constant praying all night meant I got little sleep. So in between sleeping at Yunus's I'd sleep at Denny's. This wasn't particularly ideal as there wasn't much room. The alternative was local hotels, one in particular was the Kirlangic hotel where my friends worked. Myself and Denny would often take a bottle of Raki there, get pissed and then simply take a key and crash out in one of it's many rooms. That came to an abrupt end when the owner came early one morning and me and Denny had to jump out of the second floor window!

It was early April now and workers gradually came into Marmaris and began looking for work. I had done my best to clean up Omar's and it was with relief that Hasan had come out of the army on leave for a couple of weeks. Myself, Mehmet and Hasan sat down and started making plans for the start of the season. However first we had to go and pick the chef and his brother up from Izmir. The following day Hasan, the twins and I rented a car and set off on the five hour drive. Hasan promised me we would have a day or two to have a look around the City and so as darkness rolled into Izmir so did we. For all that I had heard about how modern and metropolitan Izmir was it seemed like the district of Kadifekale, where Hasan and his family lived, had been forgotten as we meandered through narrow streets lined with whitewashed houses that resembled something I had only seen on Panorama documentaries. Hasan went on to explain that his family lived in the poor Arabic area of Izmir and as we pulled up outside of his home I began wondering why the hell I came here. Although my curiosity to learn other cultures was important to me, so was my life. To be in a place that resembled downtown Beruit in the middle of the night was pretty damn scary, but I trusted Hasan. I always felt protected when his big brother Mehmet was around.

"Paul come inside," he said as he opened the old wooden door and although he did his upmost to persuade me I felt better and safer in the car for some strange reason. "It's okay Hasan, I will sleep in the car," I told him. Although he wasn't happy about it Hasan and the twins went inside leaving me to sleep on the back seat of the car. It was 3am when I awoke absolutely freezing and I decided whatever lay beyond that door was a lot better then hypothermia so I got out of the car and ventured into the house looking for Hasan in pitch darkness. All I could hear was a woman praying and there on the floor were three bodies under a blanket. Hasan was lifting up the blanket as an invitation to join him and the twins on the floor and so I did. However the praying continued and although I dropped off a few times it seemed like an eternity before a slither of daylight broke through the windows. As I looked around the place for the source of the prayers, there sat the lad's mother in a chair repeating the same prayer over and over again. With a nervous smile I got up and decided I would venture out in search of a drink. As I opened the door and glanced at my watch it was 8.00am. The sun was glorious and from Hasan's family home I got a beautiful view of Izmir. Wow! This was indeed an impressive city. But this neighborhood, well the least said the better.

As I began to walk the street, being careful to remember my way, I was approached by some schoolchildren who must have been bemused by my obvious confusion and also curious as to know where I came from. They began an attempt to speak to me in many languages until when they finally stumbled across English I responded to their great joy. "You English? Manchester Utd?" With a polite 'yes' I carried on up the street but these kids seemed to be arriving from everywhere and by the time I reached the shop I must have had thirty kids following me. Having purchased my cola from a bemused shopkeeper I opened the shop door to find fifty or so kids all waving their English school books at me. Thankfully a police car saw my predicament and asked me where I was staying, they drove me the few hundred metres back to Hasan's house. When I opened the door, I was called to the kitchen where everyone was seated for breakfast. Having taken my place on the floor around a few sheets of newspapers, it dawned on me that this breakfast was especially for me. It was nothing new to me to sit on the floor around a newspaper with a frying pan, salad and olives. I had done it lots of times with the lads, but this time it was different I was their guest and what little money they had they had spent on making me feel welcome. For the first time I was seeing the real Islam and as I looked around I couldn't help but feel shy and somewhat embarrassed as this was not something I'd been prepared for. I was so relieved to leave the house that morning. Hasan took me for a tour of Izmir and so from a fanatical Islamic part of the city I was taken into Izmir itself and what I can only describe as a modern and cosmopolitan city. Oh and those Izmir girls! They say that Izmir girls are amongst the most beautiful in the world and that day I realised why it is said. I think my neck was sore for two days as it constantly turned to admire a bevy of stunning ladies who dressed in a way that allowed there stunning figures to complement their beauty.

Having picked up the chef and his brother we were heading back to Marmaris and it was only a few days later when the rest of the lads arrived. After a mass clear up of the kitchen and the rest of the restaurant we were now ready to take the shutters off and let Omar's come to life. And didn't she scrub up well! But time was running out until the start of the season and with so much to do it was beginning to see us all working sixteen hours a day, cleaning, painting or general preparation to get the place ready for its grand opening in a couple of weeks' time.

Our chef and I never saw eye to eye on a lot of things and the truth is I didn't like either him or his brother. So when we sat down with Mehmet to talk about the season's menus and the chef brought out of his folder a menu that he had been working on all winter, our relationship was going to get a lot more strained. His Summer 1999 Menu was entirely French! Avocat et Oeufs à la Mousse de Crabe, Mousse de Saumon et Câpres, Potage de poireaux et pommes de terre?? What the fuck? I really couldn't see Mr. Smith and his family from Rotherham tucking into a plate of Snails and Frogs legs and what's more the boss thought it was fantastic! I couldn't believe what I was hearing and seeing as the chef proudly produced more of his fanciful French Fayre. It was only after a long pause that I could no longer hold my tongue. "It's a nice menu but I'm afraid we can't use it!" was me being at my most polite. When the chef told me in Turkish to "Shut the fuck up" I dropped the politeness. "French tourists don't come to Marmaris, so who's going to eat that shit," I said raising my voice. "French food is the best food in the world, it's international," argued the chef with my boss nodding in agreement. A long and heated debate went on with me getting the help of some British reps to persuade Mehmet that this was a disaster.

The truth is, Nihad our cook, was indeed an excellent chef and without a doubt one of the best in Marmaris but he always thought he knew best and any attempt by me to offer him my advice about what British people wanted to see on a menu was always seen by him as an attack on his culinary skills. It wasn't, but like so many chefs, his head was up his arse. That was, however, only one of a few fall outs that would see us not talking again, not ever! The boss was obviously thinking he knew best as a chef and was frightened to death of losing him and rightly so. But on the other hand, if I was going to be the manager of Omar Sharif that summer then he had to back me up and, much to the anger of the Chef, Mehmet would always back me up that season. That gave me the freedom to make Omar's into something British people wanted and it allowed us to make the very best of what turned out to be a terrible season.

As quickly as they disappear at the end of summer the tourists appeared that April. The Turkish construction workers are like some sort of spawn that only appear in certain months but you can be sure that when they do appear they are in great demand. That is something that I have never quite got a grasp of, you would think that as the season ends in October the hotel and restaurant owners would start thinking about the following season. Yes they do, but I'm afraid thinking is where it stops. So for five months of the season the Turkish owners sleep, eat and sit around talking and the last thing on their mind is the following summer until April comes along then it's all systems go and everything has to be done in a month! And it's not one or two owners who think like this, no it's all of them, so there is no great demand until April for electricians, bricklayers, joiners etc. and then all of a sudden they are inundated with work so much so that they can name there own price and like it or lump it you either pay it or you don't get the work done. It has to be said though, the owners of hotels, restaurants and bars do get the jobs done (in a fashion). Yes it might be shoddy, it might be dangerous but it does get done. And my boss was a prime example of Turkish style lastminute.com with everything. Unfortunately that trait is one I picked up during my time in Turkey.

So down come the shutters at Omar's and even Denny was forgiven for his wall and was roped in to do some bricklaying, strictly sober of course, with me laboring for him. We were doing Britain proud, much to the amusement of the Turks as myself and Denny mastered the art of using primitive tools. All the staff had arrived now and I was so happy to see Steven (Mehmet) arrive from Diyarbakır together with Sado. Omar Sharif's staff for the 1999 season was complete apart from Hasan who had reluctantly returned to his military service.

I liked having Steven around, he was like my little brother and looked after me. For his nineteen years he definitely wasn't stupid. Some of the stories he told me about his childhood in Diyarbakir left me in no doubt that he had indeed lived a hard life and had to grow up pretty quick.

Even though sometimes his habits annoyed me, I don't think I would have got through that season without him.

It was now time for me to move out of Mehmet's as I learned that we were all to live together in staff quarters and the thought of fourteen of us living under one roof sent a chill up my spine. However I was pleasantly surprised to find our accommodation wasn't that bad. Well, not for me anyway, the top floor apartment was around three hundred yards from Omar's and although it was a long walk up those stairs the place had three rooms, one large front room where the waiters would sleep in four bunk beds and then a smaller room for the Chef and his creepy brother and then my room. Yes my room, all to myself and it was pretty nice with a balcony. I was made up until it came to getting a shower as we all had to share one toilet one shower and one bath which was to be only used for the washing of clothes. I was given a quick lesson on how to wash clothes in the bath. Fill bath with enough hot water to cover clothes, pour in washing powder and then jump up and down on them for ten minutes. Then rinse out into large blue bucket type container, then simply hang up on one of those Turkish clothes horses (that's if you can find room for your boxers amongst the endless array of white Y fronts and vests!!). So after going to the market where I bought myself some bedding and an ironing board, I set about making my room as cozy as possible. I have to say that first night when I got home and looked around my little room together with balcony, I though it was ideal. Although the lads did take the piss with regards to my choice of bedding and said my bedroomed reminded them of a Turkish honeymoon suite! But it was my own personal space where I could lock myself away and I loved it there, apart from the shower of course and the constant knocking on my door from the lads wanting to talk and borrow things at all times in the night. I eventually learned never to open my door and they got sick of knocking in the end. Only Steven knew our secret knock and he was welcome most of the time but even my little brother was a pain in the arse at times and used every excuse possible to get into my room.

Omar Sharif was nearly ready for the new season although with only a week to go we still didn't have the new floor Mehmet had promised and without the new floor we couldn't build the new bar so when I mentioned this to Mehmet it was like a lightbulb had come on in his head and he promised me it would be done the following day. With a whistle across the road my old friend Emin, the taxi driver came over and after some brief instructions from Mehmet he returned half an hour later in a huge tractor and proceeded to dig up the full floor of the restaurant. Amazingly one hour later we were down to bare soil and waiting arrival of the men who would lay the new marble floor. The very next day the floor was laid and it looked amazing, the new bar was also built that night, Mehmet leaving me to supervise the building work. "Paul please don't take your eyes of them," he instructed me. When I enquired as to why he told me that some other bar might offer them better money and they would simply down tools and go off to do a job for the highest bidder. So that night I sat tirelessly watching over them in case they did a runner and although the bar was hurriedly slapped together it was the best we were going to get. So here we were, two days to opening and applying the finishing touches and then we were ready. The staff kitchen had been cleaned thoroughly and food was now readily available albeit staff food it was definitely better then Denny's egg butties.

Most bars have a BBQ on the night before they open to thank everyone for the hard work getting the businesses ready and Omar's was no different. So having been to the market with Steven for the fruit and veg our BBQ would take place that very night and what a night it was! All the staff and a few guests who had worked on the place, were invited. Also holiday reps and any other people who could be influential that season. There is not a lot I can remember after a mammoth Raki fest that night but I seemed to remember Steven and I struggling up the stairs and with a hangover from hell the following morning I went to the bathroom to freshen up only to take a look in the mirror and look again in misbelieve as the following nights antics slowly came back to me. In those days, as you can see in the photographs, my hair was pretty long and although I was always complaining about it to all that would listen, I liked my hair that length, it shaded my neck from the summer sun and I thought it took five years off me. Even though I'd constantly tell everyone I would have it cut, I secretly loved it. So that morning when I looked in the mirror I was horrified to find that my hair had been completely shaved off! Apparently I promised the girls from Airtours I would get my hair cut that night and having heard it all before they instructed the staff to carry me down to the barbers where they held me down in the chair and shaved it off. The story goes that I didn't put up much of a struggle but I find that hard to believe particularly as the barber avoided me for two weeks. When I did eventually see him he ran up the street shouting his apologies!

So here I was on the opening day of the season. A new look Omar Sharif restaurant and a new hair cut for me. And didn't I look just great in my regulation staff attire which consisted of black pants and peach shirt with a black tie. All I needed was to coax my first customers into the restaurant which wasn't going to be particularly easy as there weren't many tourists around. They did however come later that week and two customers in particular were going to make my season more difficult and cause a lot of bad feeling and tension between us and our rivals Simpson's across the road.

I had heard about the reputation of the family who owned Simpson's, but to be honest I never really had any issues with them and from what I had heard I was glad I hadn't. Originating from Trabzon, a city in northern Turkey that is renowned for producing mafia style families, this family lived up to that reputation. With seven brothers, all who were in and out of prison, they were notorious down our street. Indeed three years prior their restaurant had been involved in a shooting when some local gangsters pulled up outside and started shooting indiscriminately into the restaurant wounding a couple of the brothers and a few customers who had the misfortune of being in the place at the time.

Well this particular day we had a couple of girls come into Omar's. They mentioned that they had eaten in Simpson's the night before and didn't feel well at all. When I asked if they had eaten the barbeque chicken from there they said they had. I told them that the chickens they had been eating had been spinning around on a spit since the opening day of the season. It was true, but I didn't think they would go and tell the family in Simpson's what I had said but that is what happened and the brothers made their feelings clear to me. With only ten metres of road separating me from them they would all make throat-cutting gestures to me. If I'm honest I was shitting myself! This would go on for weeks and later tension between our neighbours staff and ours would reach breaking point. I tried to ignore the intimidation and get down to work.

Unusually, Marmaris was very quiet. One of the reasons were the terrorist threats from the PKK who had threatened Turkish tourism with bombs the year before. The PKK issued statements warning people not to holiday in Turkey and these threats seemed to be working as two weeks into the season saw no real improvement. We were ticking over but just could not get our season started properly. For me being the hassle man and the manager, it meant having to work tirelessly to think of ways to encourage business. This meant me bringing our restaurant prices down, introducing a set menu and improving our entertainment. It all worked and we eventually picked up and began to fill up every night, much to the annoyance of our rivals who, I'm sure put it all down to me. Although I would like to accept the accolade of being as great a hassle man as so many people thought, the truth is I wasn't. The truth was we had a great team who worked very hard to satisfy customers. We also had a great chef and together with the great atmosphere we created, the word was again getting around that Omar Sharif restaurant was the place to be. Once tourists start seeing your restaurant full and everywhere else empty then that's the greatest advertisement of all. Plus the fact that we had the majority of reps from Sunquest and Airtours in our pockets so we were up and running and once again I was drawing attention to myself. Denny was also doing well up the road but now the season had got going I would rarely see him. Someone I did see though was Sevil and it happened by accident. A friend of mine who worked in her restaurant asked me if I could pick up a couple of his customers as they couldn't find Omar's. Off I went and there she was. All those old feelings came flooding back. After a brief smile and hello I left it at that though.

As the weeks progressed and our staff started asking about when we would be getting paid I knew it was up to me to talk with Mehmet about money. We were full every night we were taking money and quite rightly the lads wanted money to send home to their families. So myself and Mehmet started the tiresome cat and mouse financial mind games that I was now getting to be particularly good at. We had been opening the tip box and that had been paying for my cigarettes, bar bills etc. but I wanted paying, as did the staff. Morale was getting low and one day I couldn't believe my ears when Mehmet came to give me five hundred pounds and told me to take a walk with him to the centre. I did and what a surprise was in store for me. As we entered the recently opened Turkcell shop Mehmet bought me a brand-new state-of-the-art Motorola mobile with one of those cheesy cases so I could proudly show off my phone attached to my belt. I was over the moon, although some days later I wished I never had the damn thing as it meant I had no hiding places anymore. Also the old green monster I hated about Turkish people meant that everyone, including our own staff resented me for it. It was also a status symbol for Mehmet as it showed we were doing so well that he could by his staff a phone. I was one of only a few workers in Marmaris who had a mobile phone. Being the manager also meant that I was responsible for money that was coming in and going out of the restaurant which meant I had access to all waiters note pads and both me and the chef would sit down and work out percentages and who would be paid what. I was getting to know the Turkish pay structure and procedures very well. Also all the fiddling that went on and goes on in every restaurant in Marmaris like the tricks waiters tried to pull in order to pocket a customer's bill and money. Luckily it didn't go on in our restaurant but it was a good learning curve for the future. What did go on though was stealing, by the twins, and it only became apparent one night when we all played a late-night football match. Some customers came along to watch, September gave a girl his jacket to look after and she produced a fistful of foreign currency from out of his pocket. Low and behold he had somehow amassed six hundred pounds in krona, lira, dollars and pounds from somewhere and it could only have come from two places, either from the till or from the tip box. It turned out to be both. When confronted they always blamed Mehmet, their big brother, saying they were taking money from him to send home to their family in Izmir. They said that Mehmet was gambling all the money playing backgammon every day down the bazaar. They felt the takings from the restaurant didn't belong to him, it belonged to their family. But at the end of the day the fact was the twins were stealing money from the restaurant takings and the tip box, in doing so they were also taking bread out of the mouths of the staff and their families who so heavily depended on their sons sending money back home. You would have thought the twins would have learned their lesson when the chef caught them using a knife to rake out notes from the tip box and chased them both up the road with a carving knife. They were sacked the next day and Mehmet swore he would never have them back. But if I'm honest Omar Sharif needed the twins. A lot of customers came in just for them as they were undoubtably the funniest pair I'd ever met. They were crowd pullers themselves. So after a long talk with Mehmet they were taken back on but from that day on I was the only one in the restaurant who had access to the safe.

As for the drinking, well if anything my daily alcohol intake was increasing. I was having a couple of beers during the day, a small bottle of raki when I went home in the afternoon and on a night I switched to Vodka and coke. Only because there is no mistaking Raki when it's mixed with anything as it turns things cloudy so Vodka and coke was a perfect disguise. Mehmet must have known how much I was drinking though as he was ordering the spirits every day and I was drinking about one bottle a night. But he never said anything and the only inclination anyone had that I was half cut was when I was on the microphone on a night. Although my sometimes-slurred speech could be detected by anyone British (I often got comments from customers the next day). The Turks, and especially Mehmet, didn't have a clue. Drink was getting the better of me and I knew it. I always did breakfast service in a morning and simply carrying a cup of tea over to a customer needed me to use both hands as the shakes were a regular occurrence. Without making excuses, the extreme heat and not eating correctly could have also had something to do with it but my relationship with our chef was getting worse.

My usual routine in a morning was up at eight (if I had been to bed!) shower, wake the breakfast service lads up and then I'd be in Omar's for nine o'clock. Mehmet would be sat there drinking coffee and reading his paper and I would make myself a cup of tea and order my breakfast with the cook's brother who always did the morning service. That particular morning I ordered poached egg and toast and when it came to me it looked like something I wouldn't serve to my dog and I flipped taking it back in the kitchen and scraping it into the bin in front of him, now having a particularly good grasp of foul mouth Turkish I let fly, gave back as much as he could give me and stormed out across the road to Prestige Restaurant and had my breakfast there. Mehmet was fuming! But I told him I would never eat in our restaurant again, and I never did. Well not food cooked from the cook and his brother anyway.

This meant I was not eating properly at all and on top of that with the heat getting over the hundreds and putting in sixteen hour days I was killing myself. I did eventually get into a routine where Steven would cook for me during the day and Sado would make me a pizza on a night and that's basically what I lived on all season. The Pizza I would eat while outside touting, so sometimes I would leave my pizza unattended while I worked only to find the lads had eaten half of it. I got into the habit of hiding it on a chair and then pushing the chair under the table so you can imagine my horror one night when I heard an almighty commotion. One of the waiters had escorted a couple to their table and pulled out the chair for the lady to sit on and yes you guessed it, she sat down, in her best summer dress, right on top of my Pepperoni and mushroom pizza!

I wasn't going out as much as I did my first season here. I much preferred to stay local and one place in particular I would frequent was the Queen's Chinese Restaurant which was just up the road from Omar's. One of the owners there, Hamza, was a good friend of my boss and also a drinking buddy of mine. Hamza was notorious for having a drink problem but he was a great bloke. He did cause me some big problems however, one of which was that he was always coming to Omar's in an afternoon for a game of backgammon with Mehmet. They didn't play for anything serious just the odd pack of cigarettes but my boss knew of Hamza's drink problem and instructed me not to serve him any beer. Hamza never charged me anything, even the times when I'd order a Chinese meal and he never once charged me for drinks. So how could I not serve him? It was one of the things that me and Mehmet often fell out about. Hamza was a good guy and I often used to take the woman I was with into his restaurant as I knew the place was hidden away and that I could be left in peace. Unlike at Omar's where our own waiters would be in my face all the time.

One particular night though me and Hamza had a huge fall out. A girl who used to come in our restaurant started seeing Hamza and a couple of weeks after she had gone home I was sat with him and a huge table full of his customers when I told him jokingly that his girlfriend had called me the night before and said she didn't really want him but me and that he was her second choice. Now normally Hamza would have laughed this off but for some reason he went berserk and just lifted the table over and began throwing chairs around I made a quick exit and tried to avoid the Queen's for a long time. He eventually came to Omar's and apologised. You see as far as women are concerned you have no friends with the Turks. I already knew this but I really thought Hamza was different. I learned a harsh lesson that night. Women and sex come before even the best of friendships.

My boss knew of my frequent visits to Queen's on a night and wasn't happy about it at all. His philosophy was that if I had copped off with a woman and she had a friend with her I should stay in Omar's and give the staff a chance with the friend. I never did because of Yelcin our other hassle man. He would sit down with us and if the girls didn't like him, as many didn't because of his weird attitude, then Yelcin would think nothing of insulting them. I wasn't going to interfere with someone like Yelcin, he was crazy! So the best bet for me was if my girl did have a friend I would take them to Queen's where I knew Hamza was a gentlemen and left us alone.

I'd promised myself that season that I would go out of my way to not chat up women but in truth it just wasn't possible. The more I ignored them the more they came on to me and there weren't many days that went by before I had a new one. It's not something I'm proud of but just part and parcel of working in Marmaris. You might hear Turks asking each other if their season had begun yet, what they mean by that is that the season only really begins once you get your leg over! Mine had begun before the season had officially started with a Swedish woman who I cheekily took back to Mehmet's apartment in April. A couple of months into the season and I got a phone call from a girl named Jayne who was ten years my junior and who I had been seeing during my winter in the UK. She told me she was coming to Marmaris which was awkward but a couple of weeks later she arrived with her friend Michaela who was something of a looker. Having welcomed them to our restaurant the lads were around Michaela like flies around a honey pot and they all expected me to line them up with her. I knew that was going to be a major headache for me, so on their first night I took them to Bar street and ended up in Greenhouse where I bumped into the hassle man from our friend's restaurant, Prestige. As the night went on I told them I was leaving. Jayne, my girl, wanted me to come to their hotel and stay there but that just doesn't happen in Turkey. So I decided to book into a hotel around the corner from Omar's. Michaela wanted to stay in the nightclub with the lad. I told my friend where Michaela was staying and asked him to make sure she got home okay. I knew him well, his boss was a very good friend of Mehmet's so I never expected there to be a problem. The next morning as I entered Omar's I saw Michaela being consoled by my boss and immediately realised something was wrong. She explained that the previous night this guy had indeed escorted her back to the hotel but followed her up to her room and tried to rape her. What could I say? I trusted this fella and there he was brazenly working across the road as if nothing had happened whilst this poor girl's world had fallen apart! I obviously felt that I was responsible and as word spread around our restaurant Yelcin called the guy over. I then witnessed Yelcin's renowned reputation as he battered the guy senseless in the middle of the street at nine in the morning.

A couple of days went by and Michaela fell for our love rat Mico. This was causing major issues in Omar's as Yelcin thought that having defended the girl he had sole rights to her. If the truth be known she, like most other people, was intimidated by Yelcin. Even all our staff were, but me? Yeh, if I'm honest from the first day I met the guy it was obvious he had mental health problems and he was scary. But he insulted every girl he couldn't have and as Mico wasn't brave enough to tell him I felt it was up to me to approach our boss and try and make him see sense and sack Yelcin. He was losing us customers and money as well as creating a bad atmosphere in Omar's. Unfortunately Mehmet himself seemed scared of the guy.

It turned out he wasn't scared of Yelcin but as I found out later Yelcin was financing the restaurant and he had them all by balls. But not me! That very night after I heard him insult both my girlfriend and her mate I walked out and booked into a nearby hotel and was gone for almost three days until eventually they found out where I was staying and it was Yelcin himself who came and apologised. Yelcin and I had a deep understanding and until this day I still think the world of the guy. He always tried to help me and to me was great in my earlier years. Yelcin had mental health issues and I knew all about them but he was about to enter his final few days as my fellow hassle man at Omar's. After another altercation with customers a few days later he was finished. Look, hassle men who work outside in Turkish resorts need money and they need to make money for their colleagues. In his restaurant he relies on the chef and the waiters to provide a great service, they are the backbone of the restaurant and quite simply Yelcin was extremely rich, he didn't need money, he didn't need the job but used it as a vehicle to find women. From the moment I walked into Omar's on holiday two years ago I knew he was a liability. Much as I was fond of him, now the time had come to sort this out once and for all. I was assured by Mehmet his days were numbered, we didn't need his financial help anymore and if the rest of the lads weren't prepared to stand up to him I was.

With the two girls gone home I was relieved and it was back to business. Having warned our love rat Mico about making some sort of plaything out of my friend's friend he assured me he really liked her, with tongue in cheek I accepted it. The boys at Omar's knew I wasn't stupid, I knew the system and they could do what ever they wanted with other girls but I think I made it clear that week that they would never make a dick out of me by playing their games with people I knew!

I was beginning to regret having my mobile phone. There are times, as you will read later, when I needed my own space but this bloody thing attached to my belt just never gave me the space I needed. Should I leave the restaurant for longer than an hour the phone would be ringing. Sometimes it drove me crazy but on the other hand it had its advantages as I used to get calls from my friends and family back home. However I used to get another frequent caller usually late on in a night after Id finished, Sevil. She had her own place now, down by the front, and she would call me asking me to come around. Those nights stay with me forever and although she did call me when I was in some particularly awkward positions, for me, the world stopped with her. This wasn't about lust, sex or holiday romance, this was love from my heart and she still meant the world to me. I still couldn't get it into my head that the chances she took in those days meant that I meant the world to her too, but I just didn't get it then.

Marmaris was dead, but our restaurant was still full every night. It began to be a weekly occurrence now when people would stop me in the street and offer me jobs. As flattering as it was, I was staying put. One guy who never let up however was a guy called Octay. At that time he owned a restaurant up the road, Al Pacino. Mehmet actually caught him talking to me one day and told him, in no particular terms, that he was not welcome. Even Charlie, the owner of the George and Dragon across the road, eventually gave in and shook my hand one night telling me politely if I ever fancied a change then there was always a job for me there. I liked Charlie, I crucified the George and Dragon in that season. Indeed his staff used to close up at eleven and come and sit with our staff in Omar's. We were the number one on the road and there was nothing anyone could do about it. Yes the police came but, as before, Mehmet's contacts always informed us of the visits. I was getting cocky though, almost too cocky. Now being the only hassle man at Omar's I would walk the entrances to our restaurant like some sort of god. I knew that our reputation meant that anyone passing was coming directly to Omar's and I didn't really need to hassle. The tensions across the road at Simpson's was getting worse. Their father and boss used to park his car directly across the pavement on our side of the road meaning that people, potential customers, couldn't pass his car and had to cross the road. Although Mehmet had been across and talked to him nothing changed and this was beginning to get our backs up. Steven's in particular. Then one night two of the brothers actually came into our restaurant and sat with two of our female customers. This is simply not done in Turkey and because they were from a restaurant we hated this was an act of war! It got scary, really scary, to a point were Stephen and Sado together with their friends from Faulty Towers (another Kurdish family not to mess with in Marmaris but great friends of ours) would sit directly opposite Simpson's and goad the Simpson's family into confrontation. It got so bad that Mehmet was given the ultimatum that if he wasn't going to resolve the matter then Stephen and his Kurdish friends would. So Mehmet and the boss from Simpson's came to some sort of an arrangement. Although the atmosphere between our two restaurants remained like a time bomb all season. I underestimated the bravery of our staff, Steven in particular. One night I realised just how crazy he really was. I was laid in bed, it must have been around 2am, when I heard a commotion. It was Steven shouting at the restaurant downstairs to turn the music down. On investigating further I went into their room to see Steven and Sado along with a couple of our lads getting dressed. Ten minutes later the music stopped only to be replaced by the sound of smashing glasses. The next day I saw just what our staff were capable of. As I passed the restaurant in question, I could see it had been trashed. Steven was, and still is, just one of those lads you don't mess with. He's frightening! I have been so lucky to have him on my side all those years but, as you will read later, we had our fallouts too. Although I know he would have no problems in putting me in an early grave, he had, and still has, far too much respect for me.

Another thing that continued to trouble me was depression. Having suffered a nervous breakdown after my father's death in 1996 it became a daily battle to fight off this wretched illness. Although I was originally on a daily course of Prozac I never took my medication with me to Turkey. I thought my demons could not follow me. Alas my thoughts were dumbfounded as on the odd days when Turkey got the better of me I just sat on the edge of my bed and cried like a baby. A lot of people think that running away from depression makes things easier, unfortunately that's not true. İt's something I carried with me to Turkey and will probably carry it to my grave with me. Even to this day I still have my moments when the world comes crashing down on me but thankfully today my family, especially my grandson, tend to banish those feelings of hopelessness.

I could go on and on with regards to my antics and stories of that season but I didn't want to write a book about my stories as I would need a lot more time and indeed a hell of a lot hard drive space on my computer. No, I just wanted to give you a little insight into my life there. İndeed there are lots more stories to tell you as I get further on. I think you now have the jist of things so I will finish this chapter and swiftly move on. What happened next was to end my season abruptly, so I will just add one more little paragraph to sum up.

It was getting into August now and one of the hottest seasons Marmaris had seen for years. I had been to Rhodes once already with a good friend of mine Paula who was a rep for Sunquest and my early arrival in Marmaris that season meant I would have to start making plans for my second visit to renew my three month Visa. The daily battle with Mehmet for staff wages was still a ball ache. Although, at that time, I think he was only a few weeks behind with payment. Sevil and I had once again fallen out after she caught me with a girl from Finland in Hamza's place late one night. Also I had kind of fallen for another girl from Holland called Andrea. For some strange reason I fell for her because she wouldn't give into my sexual advances. I found this pretty challenging as it was a rare occurrence. I did want something I couldn't have but her words to me was I could get as much as I wanted if I ever went to Holland and we all want things we can't have right? I did eventually marry that girl in Holland but that's for later.

Marmaris was in a price frenzy trying to attract customers as the tourist season, which should have now been in full swing, was rapidly declining due to the renewed terrorist threats because the Kurdish leader, Apo Ocalan, had been captured. While restaurants were offering crazy deals to take our customers away we continued to flourish. I had not only fallen out with the Chef and his brother but with the twins after September tried to stab me with a corkscrew. I will finish with this story as, although it may seem unimportant, I want to give you an example of one of the greatest flaws in Turkish mentality. I believe you would encounter this on a daily basis if you decide to work in Turkey. This flaw, I hasten to add, is not reserved for any Turk in particular, I can quite categorically tar them all with the same brush on this occasion. That flaw is the old green-eyed monster named Jealousy. I've given you a few examples already of the run ins I've had with people in the first few chapters of this book and you will no doubt read a few more but they all have one thing in common… jealousy! Women, clothes, possessions, money, in fact anything you have that they don't and the jealousy raises its ugly head. In my case it was many, many things. My relationship with Mehmet and the trust he put in me, my wages, my clothes, my women, my mobile phone and my ability to fill our restaurant every night.

This particular day however my patience with the twins finally broke.

Football shirts are a possession that most holidaymakers take on holiday with them and thanks to the generosity of many of our customers we had hundreds of them hanging around the restaurant. But we had one particular customer from Middlesboro who was sporting the new blue and white Boro top and I wanted it! Not for the restaurant but for myself. Unfortunately so did the twins. So I bought a bottle of Raki one night and got the fella drunk and with a bit of persuasion, at the end of the night he promised the shirt to me before he left the following day. To be honest I never expected to see him again, but true to his word the following day the fella came in and tossed the shirt to me. I was genuinely appreciative and slipped it on proudly. September wasn't impressed and I could see by the way he was looking at me that he was angry. I'd seen that face many times before so I paraded around in it a bit more rubbing his nose in it. Then he simply flipped picking up a corkscrew from the bar and putting a huge tear in the back of the shirt. I responded by picking up a chair and throwing it at him. After a brief scuffle it settled down before his brother and twin, October, accused me of stealing from the restaurant and it's staff. He had come to this conclusion because I had started 'Play your cards right' in Omar's at the start of the season. Yes I was making money on it, but apart from a packet of fags the money went towards a rolling jackpot which sometimes reached two hundred pounds. This meant that come nine o'clock every night, when all other bars and restaurants in the area were empty, Omar Sharif was jam packed with people eager to win that jackpot. Everyone understood my philosophy that 'play your cards right' was bringing the restaurant food and drink revenue. However the twins genuinely believed I was pocketing huge amounts of profit from it. So he joined his brother in an attack on me. This ended up involving all the staff and our restaurant erupted into a mass brawl. I took the huge board advertising 'play your cards right' and threw it in the skip outside. For the first time the staff at Omar's were at loggerheads with each other and although, with Steven by my side, the staff stood by me, things were never the same. Perhaps what happened a couple of days later was a blessing in disguise. But my message is, please don't underestimate the jealousy thing, it could get you into a lot of trouble. I know this might sound difficult and somewhat overboard it's not. İf you ever work in Turkey keep your personal business to yourself and never take your personal matters to work. Keep work issues and colleagues separate from what you do outside of work and never try to mix the two as it will end in tears.

So as I lead up to the next chapter I will finish on a lighter note. As you can imagine I have seen thousands of holidaymakers come and go but few I could actually call friends. However one particular group of lads that summer were what I would call fantastic and a credit to their country. Six strapping lads from Newcastle used to grace our restaurant every night. Although they could get quite loud and boisterous the lads were no bother whatsoever. One of the lads, 'Dougy', was a tall good-looking lad from Whitley bay. Now I used to have many holiday reps visit me but one in particular, who we shall call Sarah, worked for Thompsons. I had seen her antics with Turks over the season so it was refreshing to see her take a fancy to Dougy. İt seemed that, after a chance meeting in Omar's one night, these two had fallen for each other. So as Dougy's final day approached he told me he really wanted to stay on in Marmaris to be with Sarah. He asked me for a job and at the time I thought it was a great idea. There were many Geordies in Marmaris and with Yelcin getting the sack I was working the door by myself. I felt that with another Brit on the door we would attract more customers. Although we didn't particularly need another hassle man I was tired and needed a bit of a break and loved the thought of another Brit to work alongside of me. So I put the idea to Mehmet who refused point blank. So I put it to him about him being a Geordie he would bring other Geordies into the restaurant. Eventually, much to Dougy's and Sarah's delight it was agreed we would give him a week's day by day trial. Now Dougy may have been many things but he definitely wasn't a hassle man and I quickly came to the conclusion that he never would be. Although I tried every trick in the book to encourage him to talk with potential customers outside, he couldn't I'm afraid. I liked the guy and came up with a novel idea. I would cut my breaks in an afternoon and work extra hard to get customers in on a night and it worked. I told Mehmet that all these new customers had been touted by Dougy. All the lads in the restaurant knew the truth and I think so did Mehmet, but we got away with it. İn my arrogance, one thing that didn't cross my mind that August was that other restaurants could maybe tolerate one British worker at Omar's but two? Never in a million years!

5

The Hotel California

The only difference to this particular night was that all the staff at Omar's were proudly wearing our new staff attire. And what a bonny bunch we looked in our salmon shirts, black ties and sensible black pants that blended in so well with our new tablecloths, some would call it cheesy, I would just call it Turkey. I had originally thought the outfit was only for the waiters but apparently not. So for me it was out with jeans and designer shirts and in with clothes I wouldn't have been seen dead in back home. After a few sarcastic wolf whistles from our British customers, I ventured to my door to begin a night's hassling. It must have been around ten o'clock when I first noticed something strange. As one scruffy looking old Turk passed me a couple of times I just had a funny feeling something was wrong and then I saw a car pull up and our boss Mehmet told me to sit down which I did with a family from Sheffield and a beer was put in front of me. This was not unusual as we often had scares but when I saw the cars occupants get out and start talking with Mehmet I knew something was very wrong. Mehmet was a man who rarely showed emotion but the look on his face told me I was in deep, deep trouble. I tried in vain to blend in with the surroundings alas it was to no avail as these two guys who stood at the entrance talking to Mehmet knew who they wanted. At one point it did cross my mind to sneak out the back way but they had their eyes fixed on me; my salmon shirt did little to offer me any form of camouflage. Then I was summoned to a concerned Mehmet.

"Paul, you have to go with these men," was all I was told. These guys had unfinished business and I heard them ask Mehmet for the guy in the white shirt and poor Dougy was given up to these guys as well. We were both guided into the back of the unmarked police car. All that was going through my mind at the time was pity for Dougy, I had gotten away with it for a season, Dougy only a week or so. I had grown accustomed to the way things are done in Turkey. Dougy didn't have a clue, I tried to console. Things were looking pretty ominous for us as, unbeknown to me, everyone who gets locked up in Turkey has to go to the hospital for a check up first as Turkish jails are not known for being the most hospitable of places. Bruises seem to appear on one's body for no apparent reason! So a check up before and upon release can ascertain whether you have been involved in any incident whilst held in custody and that incident has led to the shit being kicked out of you! So glad I wasn't aware of this at the time as I had a fear of hospitals, blood tests and injections. I had more to worry about as we were led into the hospital reception and told to sit down.

In hindsight, whenever I was in trouble Denny seemed to be involved one way or another. So it should have come as no surprise when five minutes later the door opened and in he walked! He too had a fellow prisoner with him, a girl called Carol who worked at the Villa Dreams and had been working in Turkey longer then all of us. She was someone I had tried to avoid as she was, let's say, a little crazy. It must have been one of mine and Denny's fall out periods as he never said a word to me as he took his place in the reception awaiting our medicals. In the meantime I was frantically trying to get a signal on my mobile so I could call my parents back home but it was to no avail. Thankfully my panicky thoughts of injections and blood tests were quickly banished as I entered the room. I was just told to strip to my boxers and was checked over then signed a form to say I was in good health (at least that's what I thought it said). Then it was back into the police car. As if I wasn't having a bad enough night as I tried in vain to confirm my story that I was merely a holidaymaker something else happened. We took the road from Armutalan to Marmaris police station and what happened next seemed to sum my night up. We were heading back in the direction we came and as we approached the traffic lights outside Omar's the traffic lights turned to green so obviously we stopped (red is to go in Turkey isn't it?) in full view of all the customers in our restaurant who were still intrigued as to what was going on. They saw me in the back of the car and like some sort of paparazzi frenzy they all poured out of the restaurant blocking the police car and started shouting my name and taking photographs. Finally when we moved on the policeman in the passenger seat turned to me with a smile on his face and enquired "So you don't work here eh?" Gotcha!

I don't really know what was going through my mind as we approached the bazaar and Marmaris police station as you simply cannot rule out any possibilities in Turkey. I did have faith in my boss though and his knowledge of how to bribe anyone who stood in his way. As we were led into the station Mehmet was already there. After assuring everything was okay he promised me that we would be out the next day. Then he was asked to leave. So there we were, alone and vulnerable at the mercy of the Marmaris police force. Most of whom I knew as they had been my customers during the winter months when they used to frequent Omar's to watch the football (and I cheekily used to sell them beer at a profit!). But this seemed to have nothing to do with the local constabulary, the guys dealing with us were of the plain clothed variety and pretty scary. We were led to a little room no bigger then 10ft by 6ft which was sparsely furnished with one bookshelf, minus the books, and four chairs and I have to say I was pleased that two of these plastic chairs were already taken by Denny and Carol. After a five minute pause Denny's renowned stubbornness broke and he spoke. "Suppose we are going to have to speak to each other now eh bonny lad." Then, as if the floodgates had opened, we spent the next hour discussing endless scenarios and possible outcomes. Denny had been here before two years prior and thought he knew what to expect but no-one could have predicted those next long four days. With the time getting to the early hours I needed to sleep and as it seems we were going to be in that room for the night I looked around for possible places to bed down. It was either the floor or the bookcase and I'm sure if you ask Denny about it now he will tell you that to everyone's amusement I managed to lay out on the shelf and drift into a heavy sleep. Denny informed me later that he was taking bets on how long it would be before I fell out of my temporary bed. I never did!

I woke to the sound of broken English and any hangover İ ever had was unusually inferior to the pain in my neck from the bloody bookcase. As on any other given day, İ needed tea and a fag. Unfortunately I was to be granted neither as we were asked to approach the desk sergeant to log in and surrender our possessions. Later on they would also take our passports. Mehmet walked in looking like a man on a mission all suited up together with Denny's boss Tefik from Paradise restaurant. Without saying a word they went straight through to the Chief's office. Through the glass door we could see Mehmet waving his arms about frantically in typical Turkish sign language that speaks so much louder than words. I could almost read it myself as Mehmet often used this when he was angry with the staff at Omar's. Fifteen minutes later he emerged not looking like he had got the result he had expected and we were told we could sit outside in the front for a while. So with Mehmet sending someone for Turkish tea he began to explain that we indeed had a problem. This wasn't a matter that Marmaris or indeed Mugla police could deal with. İt had come from Ankara and basically we had to wait and see what the day would bring. But Mehmet assured me he was doing his best and that we should be out by the end of the day. I believed him, well I had little choice did I. After Mehmet left, and I had my tea and fags, we were ushered inside again. Not to our little room this time. İt was for real we were going to officially be prisoners and with no more ado myself, Denny and Dougy were marched into a cell, the door slammed shut and with a turn of the key my heart sank. I think it was about that time that I realised my season was well and truly over. Mehmet could usually wave his magic wand and get anything he wanted but not even he could get me out of this mess and that scared the shit out of me! As I sat down on the wire benches that surrounded the cell I was scared, real scared. Looking around, the cell was no bigger than your average bedroom. With one small window allowing a faint bit of light to pass through, it was dark, damp and stunk to high heaven of sweaty bodies. There was nowhere to wash, no toilet, in fact nothing, nothing at all. This is when Denny started reeling out the first sentence to 'I Spy'. I just cracked up laughing. I didn't want Dougy to see I was weak; I had been his mentor since coming to Marmaris and felt guilty for getting him into this mess. So for the next few hours we just spent the time laughing. God knows what they thought of us in there, but as the sun came up that morning so did the heat in there. As midday approached, we were roasting and sweat was literally dripping from us. Then a face appeared that, at the time, wasn't a welcome one for me and Denny and a probable suspect as to who had informed… Octay or Paul as he liked to be called. At the time he had the Al Pacino restaurant which was down our street and we had been warned many times that he was calling the police and reporting us but we just let it go over our heads as another idle threat. Octay knew Carol more than he knew Denny and I as she used to work for him. Now, however, she seemed even less pleased to see him than we did. Carol, being a female, couldn't be locked up with males so due to the fact that there was only one cell she was allowed to sit in the corridor. Octay had come up to see her and as he went past us he passed in a small bottle of water through the cell hatch. For as much as we loathed him this was a godsend because we were baking in there, and I mean baking!

All was quiet outside apart from the odd visitor but we were told we would be let out for an hour to eat later on that night. It was nice to see so many faces turn up to offer their support bringing with them food from their various establishments. So instead of the bread and water the desk sergeant told us we would be eating whilst we were in there, with one middle finger pointing firmly upwards to him, we ate like kings. Kebabs, sandwiches and pizza were on the menu that night and we were looked on with disdain as we tucked into our fayre. We did offer what we couldn't eat to the coppers sat guarding us though.

Although Mehmet came to see us that night this time there were no promises of freedom. We came to the conclusion that we were in the hands of the officials and in Turkey that was a rather precarious situation to be in. So it was back off to our cell and a long, long night lay ahead as from two o'clock the doors would open hourly and every criminal who offended in Marmaris that particular night would be hurled in to the cell with us. I was awoken by the sounds of crying and getting up to investigate I peered through the grill in the door to see four Kurdish boys lined up. They were in the process of being slapped senseless by two plain clothed coppers. The boys, no older than twenty, were literally crying like babies as this beating seemed to go on for hours. A firm bang on the grill meant that I was not a welcome witness to the event so I promptly tried again to sleep. Dougy was laid opposite me and I tried to comfort him, it was quite clear that he couldn't handle the situation.

As word spread about our predicament the visitors gained in numbers as did the food. But that morning I needed tea and literally begged the young guy behind the desk to let me order some tea. He didn't but came to the compromise that I could go myself but would be closely guarded. So off I went into the bazaar with my escort and his sub machine gun. When I got back we sat in the garden at the front. Myself, Denny, Dougy and Carol, the regular visitors Mehmet Tefik, Sarah (Dougy's girlfriend) Steven and a couple more reps. Also the boss from Faulty Towers who, it seemed, was getting more information than anyone and told us that we would go to the courthouse that day and that the British Embassy would come to see us before we went in.

Around three o'clock I heard the door unlock and the guard beckoned me to follow him upstairs. There sat a lady who was from the British Embassy. She could give me no answers whatsoever and two minutes later I was marched across the road to the courthouse with Mehmet. Again given no answers and didn't even know what I was being charged with. But when I saw Mehmet hand over a pile of money I saw some light at the end of the tunnel and presumed this was the end of the matter. It wasn't though, not by a long chalk. Now as an official prisoner I was taken down to İçmeler police station to be fingerprinted again. Then I was back in the cell and

Denny's jokes were simply not funny anymore. I did, however, like the one about the huge cockroaches in the cell running away with Dougy's shoes! My temper was beginning to burn on a very low fuse though and I needed a drink. So when Sarah asked me what I would like bringing that night I requested a bottle of Fanta and instructed her to pour half of the contents out and fill it with vodka. Talk about contempt. I knew that every night the entire supply of Marmaris's electricity would be cut off and during those few minutes when the lights went out I was going to consume the entire bottle. Sarah was as good as her word and without saying a word to anyone when the lights went out so did mine! I remember waking up the next day with an almighty hangover and Denny smiling at me. He went on to explain that when the lights came back on I was under the table and begging the Turkish police to put me back in the cell. Then for the rest of the night I treated the entire station to a night with Frank Sinatra as I belted song after song of Frank's classics much to the amusement and disbelief of the Marmaris police force.

Day three in the Hotel California, as we called our temporary home, and we were unexpectedly woken up early and were told we were being released. However nothing is simple in Turkey and on meeting Mehmet outside he told us we would be taken to the harbour where we would get the Hydrofoil to Rhodes get our Visa stamped and then come back to freedom the following day. So it was back to the hospital to get checked over on release and as we left the police station we were bid farewell by the coppers. I'm sure they were as relieved as we were that they wouldn't be seeing us again. After the hospital we found ourselves waiting at the harbour for the hydrofoil to arrive. When it appeared on the horizon that red-hot summer afternoon we were already contemplating our first pint when we got on board. The nearer it got the thirstier we got and then she docked. As we waited patiently in the queue with our boarding cards at the ready all hell broke loose. Carol, for reasons known only to her, had done a runner and we were taken and held in the harbour master's office. Half an hour later we were informed they had found her hiding in the back of a taxi but that was it, we would not get that long awaited Efes, we would not go to Rhodes, the only place we were going was back to the Hotel California to spend or third night as prisoners! As we walked into the station both our police escorts and their colleagues down at the Marmaris nick were in fits of laughter. By now my head was about to explode and I was in no mood for laughter. Still wearing the same stinking clothes I'd had on for the past three days we were back in our cell and locked up. However, I was told afterwards that Carol had done us a huge favour as, yes, we would have boarded the hydrofoil but once we had got to Rhodes we would never have been granted re-entry to Turkey and we would have been stuck in Greece with no money, none of our possessions and with no chance of getting back to Turkey. I didn't know this at the time and the unfortunate Carol was feeling the full force of my temper as it seemed everyone was looking to me and my boss to get us out of the pile of shit that we were in. I had had enough and made myself quite clear when I declared that from that moment on there would be no more antics. It was each man for themselves although I was responsible for Dougy and wouldn't rest until I had got him back to the UK. I used to hear him crying in the night and it made me stronger and more determined. The following day was spent pretty much the same and our ever-increasing visitors were becoming tiresome to our guards. It seemed that our fourth night in the Hotel California would be our last as we had heard it on the grapevine that the next day we would be released and taken to Dalaman for deportation. I wasn't going to believe anything I heard though and only accepted it when I had it confirmed later that night by the authorities that we were indeed leaving the next day. We would stay in police custody until they put us on the plane and we needed to start thinking about organizing flight tickets. Hopefully this night really would be our last one.

The following morning saw the place full of visitors who had heard of our imminent release. They came to say their farewells because for all intense and purposes deportation meant a red stamp on our passport that would exile us from Turkey for six whole years. Therefore we wouldn't see our friends again for a long, long time, if not forever. Getting the tickets wasn't a problem for us as we were in good hands with the Sunquest girls. However paying for them was another thing, my pre-season promises of saving money had not materialised and I was broke apart from a couple of hundred pounds in my bank account. No-one at home could help me because they didn't know of my predicament so Mehmet would have to pay for them. I say them because Dougy needed a ticket too. Being the respectful boss he was we didn't need to ask and the tickets for a one o'clock flight to Manchester had been paid for. So after another sleepless night we were allowed out and going into my fifth day without a shower I asked if I could clean up and change somewhere. I had a strip wash at a small sink and got changed (Steven had brought my case from my apartment with some clean clothes). So, there we were sat in the garden in the morning sun with visitors arriving by the minute until the front garden of the police station was full of well wishers. The police soon lost their patience though and to our disbelief locked us up again informing us that when our visitors left we could be on our way to Dalaman. Good fortune was in my favour that morning as I had signed for my mobile so I called Steven from the cell to tell him to thank everyone but they must go home. By now it had quietened down, in fact the only voice you could hear was Mehmet's informing the police that unless we went now we would miss our flights. Their answer was simple, "So what, they will have to go later and buy another ticket." Eventually we were allowed to leave into our waiting transfer vehicle. If you could just imagine the four of us together on the backseat with our entire belongings in the boot and on our knees and in the front was the taxi driver and an armed policeman. We were late and didn't stop for one green light and we made it to Dalaman in record time. Although still an hour late we were informed that they were holding the plane up for us like we were VIPS or something. Now came the next problem. My visa never was an issue it had always been in date as obviously was Dougy's. However Denny was out by about a year and Carol about three. But as they were that busy trying to get us through customs etc. they didn't bother to check properly. Denny got through but I'm afraid Carol didn't.

And that, I'm afraid to say, was the last I ever heard of her. But Carol, if you are reading this I still have your iron!

As we were led through all the checkpoints and up the stairs at gunpoint our fellow passengers must have wondered who the bloody hell we were. If initially they were under the impression we were someone important I'm sure the theory was quickly ruled out when they saw the state of us. 'Good afternoon ladies and gentlemen, I'm your pilot' Denny announced to them, but I'm afraid the hour delay meant the passengers were in no mood for jokes, neither was I as I took my seat alongside Denny and Doug. Then came the moment of truth as I looked over to Denny and we opened our passports simultaneously. To our astonishment they hadn't red stamped our passports, God knows why, but they hadn't and now it was time to celebrate. When the beer trolley came around I thought briefly about Mehmet, he had given me four hundred pounds to come home with and I had a drink for him. Together with Denny we had a drink to just about anybody!

Many things were going through my mind on that long haul back to Manchester. Although, to be honest, I wished the flight could have taken a long enough time to be able to answer all the questions I was asking myself. My unexpected early departure left me in a bit of a quandary. Where would I live and work, would I ever work in Turkey again? I also thought about how I never got the chance to say goodbye to my friends, especially Sevil, and explain my sudden disappearance. Apparently news of our imprisonment and release was hot gossip around Marmaris though so they soon found out. But I would have liked to explain things myself. However I knew one thing, for me to go back there as a worker would be way too dangerous and maybe I should call it a day and concentrate on a normal life back home, easier said then done…

What the three of us must have looked like going through arrivals, unshaven, unwashed and pissed. But as we sat in the arrival bar for a farewell pint we reflected and laughed about the past few days, it could have all been a nightmare but unfortunately the stench from our clothes told me it wasn't. Then it was time to say goodbye to my two friends. When I enquired as to what they would do now I was in total disbelief to hear Denny inform me that they would be boarding the very next flight and heading back to Marmaris! And that is indeed exactly what they did! Denny walked around Manchester all night in his shorts and then flew out to Dalaman the very next day. He was, in fact, back in Marmaris before I had even started out on my short journey back to Hull.

Myself? Well I called a transfer company in Hull and asked them to pick me up on their next available minibus at Terminal two. As I sat and waited on the couch next to the meeting point I thought it would be a good idea to crack open a bottle of Raki that I had bought on the plane. After drinking a good amount of it I promptly fell asleep. I woke up some hours later and had another few drinks, and again fell asleep. This went on until the bottle was finished. Although I was awoken many times by airport security I explained I was waiting for a transfer and when I finally came out of my coma it was two days later!! I then had the bare face cheek to ring the transfer company up and furiously ask them where the hell they were. After offering their apologies they said they had been several times and even called me on the airport tannoy. I was back in Hull in no time. My Mam was surprised to see her somewhat disheveled son turning up on her doorstep, but she welcomed me back with open arms and a thousand questions, some of which I never did answer. But Mam I'm sure you will be reading this book and I hope this chapter has put closure to the matter.

6

Home Is Where the Heart Is?

Hull, a city in East Yorkshire, which was once a thriving fishing port, but is now more famous for its single span suspension bridge over the river Humber. With one major road in and one out it's at somewhat of a dead end so visitors are rare. To go there you must have a good reason and unfortunately these days Hull doesn't have a lot to offer visitors. With its very own unique accent my Hullensians can spot outsiders a mile off. Although, as with all Yorkshire folk, its inhabitants have a warm welcome to offer, it's a clicky place where anywhere outside a twenty mile radius is considered the end of the universe. Having said that I was born and bred there and have many great childhood memories of the place. Fortunately my step dad was a travelling contractor so summer holidays meant an escape from Hull and a glimpse into how people survive without it. To many of Hull's inhabitants this is unthinkable! The fact is people from Hull don't want to leave the place. They genuinely think that venturing outside of the city's boundaries is like exploring the Amazon and to actually move out of the area you must have gone insane!

My first week back was a lucky one. My best friend Karl, who was a pub manager, had recently become the manager of what was considered the best pub in Hull. My return was a timely one as he was looking for a barman and obviously with my experience in the trade he offered me a job. Although I was planning on living at my Mam's for a while I spent more time living with Karl at the smart little apartment on the newly revamped Hull Marina that came with the job. Only my deep dark Turkish tan told people I had been away. Apart from family and friends no-one had even noticed I had spent the last two years in Turkey so I quickly settled into the normal routine of everyday life back home. Looking back, I wish they would have red stamped my passport as the novelty of being back home was rapidly wearing off and it began to be an everyday battle to get Marmaris out of my mind. İf they had have exiled me for six years then I would have known there was no way back. But while I still had my passport and my contacts in Marmaris my return was always a possibility. Of course the only thing stopping me was the chance that I could be caught again and next time the punishment would be far greater. But while that door of opportunity was open I still could not put a return to the back of my mind. İn truth, after a short while back in Hull, I realised that although this was my home town it wasn't my home. I didn't want to be there I wanted to be back in Turkey. İt could have been Hull, New York, Paris or Amsterdam İ was in, it wouldn't have mattered where, Marmaris was my home and I began to miss it so much.

Days became weeks and weeks became months. I was beginning to hate the predicament I had found myself in but İ was forcing myself to settle down and began seeing Jayne, the girl that visited me in Marmaris. Although I thought the world of her she knew that my struggle to settle down was now to involve her as she tried so hard to keep my mind away from Turkey, so much so that just after Christmas she used her money to rent and furnish a flat for us both and we moved in together. At last I had some stability. A job, a girlfriend, a home and the ability to spend time with my family and children again. Deep down though I knew this wasn't enough and I think Jayne did too. I was also still in contact with the Dutch girl who had been to Omar Sharif's the previous summer. I had promised her I would pay her a visit. So with no more ado I gave Jayne some excuse and jumped on the Hull to Rotterdam Ferry. My Dutch lady was waiting for me at the other end. She was an extremely attractive lady and now without the distraction of her holiday and my work I would spend a week with her in Tilburg. There was something about her I wanted. She was independent, strong-willed and she loved me. But did she love the real me or the me who entertained her in Marmaris where drink-fuelled fun and excitement was an everyday occurrence? She assured me on my departure a week later, she loved the real me and I left Holland knowing she was sincere in her words. I also left promising her I would be back two months later. In truth I knew I wouldn't be in Holland nor would I be in that lovely little flat back in Hull with Jayne. I knew where I would be. I just had to find a way to get back home to Marmaris somehow.

Then it came out of the blue just after a lovely Valentine's meal with Jayne. A phone call from a voice I instantly recognised as Denny. He told me his winter story on how he had left Paradise restaurant and gone to work for some brothers who had a restaurant on the beach. I heard a

Turkish voice in the background prompting him before Ihlan, his new boss, spoke to me. He explained that he had seen me work the previous season at Omar Sharif's and he and his brother were impressed. He then went on to offer me a job working at his bar/restaurant on the beach. They had heard about me being deported but assured me that I would have no problem working for them as I would be getting a work visa that would allow me to work in Turkey legally. He also explained that the job would come with a nice apartment and a good salary. I had to come to learn that what a Turkish boss promises and what they actually deliver are two different things. I had also learned the power of mind games in Turkish negotiations so Immediately turned down the offer even though he had just removed the one obstacle that was blocking my return. He had also taken away all hopes of me settling down. But he had given me hope of a return to Marmaris and I knew that he would call again and that again I would turn him down. Over the next couple of weeks Denny called me four or five times. My decision had been made the first time he called me but I wanted to know just how much Ihlan thought I was worth to him. So I held out until he asked me to come over for a holiday and take a look at the set up and then decide. Without committing myself to him I planned on going to Marmaris knowing that I would accept the job but wanting to get as much out of Ihlan as possible. My next problem was how would I tell my friends, family and Jayne? If I'm honest with myself I was a coward. I couldn't bring myself to tell Jayne and simply disappeared one day in April and I haven't seen her since. I'm not going to say it was a difficult decision, what I will say is it was probably the shittiest thing I have ever done to anyone in my life! But unless you have worked or lived in Marmaris you will not understand the pure addiction of the place. As for my family and friends, I told them I was going on holiday but as I set off once again down the M62 to Manchester it felt like I was going home.

The apprehension and panic I was feeling as I approached Dalaman passport control was surely visible. With two arrests and a deportation on my record it would only take a few taps in the computer to see I had somewhat of a history and maybe I would not be allowed entry. All sorts of things were going through my mind that day but having cleared customs I was picked up by my driver and on the way back down to Marmaris with a four pack of efes to welcome me home. Towards the end of the journey, as we approached the apartments in Armutalan, a small district on the outskirts of Marmaris, there waiting for me was my old mate Denny. With a smile on his face, it seemed an eternity since I left him in that bar in Manchester airport. He welcomed me and showed me around the place. Club Sera were small, low budget apartments with a bar and a swimming pool. They were run by a family called the Ozturks. There were four brothers, Ihlan, who also owned the restaurant where I would work, Ihsan who ran a small travel agency, Mustafa who ran the apartments and the youngest brother Gullum. The family, until recently, had owned an electrical shop in Marmaris before opening a small restaurant called Al Pacino's. It had been one of our competitors down the street at Omar Sharif's and it was where Carol used to work a few seasons ago. I had heard many bad stories about Al Pacino bosses from her so I was pretty wary. However I now knew I could get back into Turkey okay so was under no pressure to committing myself to anyone. I knew I could find work anywhere, my options were open. So with this in mind I decided if I didn't like what they had to offer then I would simply go and work for someone else. I was quietly impressed with the place though. As Denny took me to my apartment I was more then pleased to see what accommodation they were offering me. Two rooms, cooking facilities and a nice balcony with a view over Marmaris. Yeah I could see me staying here I thought as I opened the balcony doors. While I smiled contently to myself a bloody wasp came down from a nest on the roof and stung me, much to Denny's amusement.

So far so good. İ spent a couple of days of holidaying and going around meeting old friends. Yunus, who was still working at a bank on the Marina, Mikail, Mehmet and Steven who, I had learned had met an English holiday rep when Id been deported the previous season and had bought his own bar. The one place I did try and avoid was my old restaurant. I didn't particularly want my ex boss Mehmet to know I was back in Marmaris to work for someone else. I would explain to him in time but now wasn't the right time as I just knew he wouldn't like the thought of me working elsewhere. İn a way I did feel guilty but what could I do? Going back to work at Omar Sharif would be a recipe for disaster and far too dangerous. As much as I wanted to pay my old place a visit I couldn't. I must admit I did pass it a couple of times for old times sake and smiled to myself as all those great memories came flooding back.

I was summoned to a meeting at the Sera Beach restaurant where we would discuss my employment. So after a few beers I ventured down there and again I was impressed by the place. Three times the size of Omar Sharif, I knew of its reputation already. I had passed it a couple of times over the years and it was a busy place, always bouncing at midnight and judging by the amount of equipment in the DJ box and the lightshow I could see why. This wasn't your two hundred and fifty quid set up like the one we had at Omar Shrif, this was a dance bar and I would have to learn pretty quick if I was to master all that equipment before I started the job. So we sat around the table and as I looked around there was one face at the table that I knew well, Octay! The guy I was convinced of informing on us to the police! Then I started putting the pieces together. Octay often walked past Omar's asking me if I fancied working for them but he was told by my boss on numerous occasions to stop trying to hassle me. Octay, was the manager at Al Pacino, Ihlan was the owner. Not only that Octay was married to the family's sister so they were related. I think Denny purposely avoided mentioning the fact about Octay being involved with the running of Sera Beach as he knew my dislike for him. When I caught his eye that night as we sat around the table Denny smiled and was greeted by a frown from myself. I felt I had been deceived. Even so I listened to what they had to offer albeit somewhat apprehensively.

Staff and Management at Sera Beach

A late night business meeting with Mikail and Mehmet from River Jewellery

Soup kitchen with the lads from Sera Beach

Me (blue shirt) getting the party started at Sera Beach

They wanted me to DJ and run the karaoke for them, nothing else. For that they would pay me six hundred pounds a month plus my apartment and food. So their offer was on the table. When I looked at it this was one hell of an offer. But with Turkish mentality kicking in I countered their offer by asking for more money and a percentage of the tip box. This didn't go down too well but I wasn't there to be popular. I was there because they wanted me. And so, with a lot of Turkish swearwords thrown in, the family huddled together and talked and talked and talked some more before telling me they would give me more money but the tip box was not on the agenda. To this I calmly got up and walked out telling them I would give them an answer the following day.

Having endless amounts of spare time, negotiations and haggling are just part and parcel of everyday life in Turkey. They love it and these discussions can go on for weeks, if not months. Have you ever gone shopping with a Turk? Us British guys think it's bad enough taking the wife shopping for a pair of shoes but shopping with these guys is like extracting your own teeth and something I try and avoid at all costs as I learnt my lesson in ninety eight whilst accompanying Hasan to buy that pair of shoes. I have slipped up a few times since when the occasion meant I had to be there as we were buying equipment for the restaurant. That first time going with Hasan back in my first season though was up there amongst the most painful experiences of my life. At the time what surprised me even more was that the shopkeepers went through the process with him without batting an eyelid as if it was a well rehearsed ancient ritual or something. I was amazed that the guys in the shoe shops didn't throttle him. Now, years later I accept this as the norm while shopping Turkish style but one part of the culture I really didn't want to embrace. I have got to admit though the Turks way of doing business is quite unique as it's rare that the full money ever gets paid immediately. Business is done more with installments promises and handshakes and the drinking of plenty of çay (Turkish tea) to keep things calm. Please if you get chance to see two Turks doing business do pay attention. İt's an art form. These guys can sit opposite each other for ages without even talking. My old boss Mehmet was a professor of negotiations and would drag me into conversation over my wages that saw me demanding money from him immediately only to see him cleverly let it drag on for weeks without me noticing. I learned a hell of a lot from him. He was a grandmaster but being a pretty good chess player myself I soon learned the art of cornering him when he tried to use his stalling tactics on me. İndeed it was me who all the staff got to approach Mehmet when it neared payday. I had learned the Turkish ways of negotiation well and was now using it for my benefit.

I carried on for a couple of days as if I was on holiday. The ball was firmly in my future employer's court and I was in no rush and it appeared that they were playing the same game as nothing was mentioned. So I used the time to relax and spend time with friends. I also had another obstacle to overcome. I had a visitor one night and although I had been expecting it I still was one I could do without. September one of the twins from Omar Sharif came to see me and after polite greetings he delivered the news I had been expecting, Mehmet wanted to see me that night at his house. So later in the evening I found myself having a couple of beers for Dutch courage before going to his house and I really didn't know what to expect. I had only felt Mehmet's wrath once when I was late for work one night and didn't like it one bit. I had seen many people on the receiving end of his anger and it wasn't pleasant. I wasn't frightened of him that night as I walked up those stairs, I knew how the conversation was going to go and that my respect and feelings for him as a person weren't going to come into it. He would only want one thing from me and that was something I wouldn't be able to give him. When he opened the door to me, I knew he meant business. I walked inside and took my seat only to hear Mehmet plead with me to go back and work for him. I knew it was not possible and although he really knew I couldn't go back there I think he just hated the idea of me working for someone else. When his pleasant pleas came to no avail, he turned nasty and told me that if I worked for anyone else in Marmaris then he would inform the police and have me arrested. I knew he was quite capable of doing that but I had a card up my sleeve and informed him that I would be getting a work visa. His smiles told me that he thought I was calling his bluff. He went on to tell me that I was like a brother to him and reminded me of all the things he had done for me. He was right, indeed he was my mentor, my rock and a person who, I had no doubt, thought the world of me. This was business though and I reminded him just what I had done for him too and that this wasn't personal and if he did infact love me like a brother he would allow me to move on. It appeared he wouldn't and his threats got louder and he resorted to trying to intimidate me. When I could take no more, I simply stood up and walked out and with him bellowing obscenities he slammed the door behind me. Would he inform the police? No. I genuinely believed that Mehmet didn't have a bad bone in his body and for me thankfully his bark was far worse than his bite!

A couple of nights later I started work at Sera Beach and I just knew it was going to take some time to adjust to working with my new colleagues. These lads had worked there together for a couple of seasons and I could tell they were apprehensive about me. But I took no shit and never would. I would let my work do the talking. Sure enough after they saw how I worked they seemed to warm to me. I knew though there was a line and they shouldn't cross it and one night I demonstrated just how far I could be pushed. The Turks have a terrible habit of interfering and when I arrived for work one night having spent the previous week arranging the DJ Box and setting up the equipment to my own desired settings I found someone had been up there and changed everything and with no more ado I informed the management that I wouldn't be working that night and simply walked out. I have mentioned in a previous chapter the important of standing your ground in Turkey. If they can't get their own way with you they might sulk for a couple of days but they will come around eventually. Draw a line and never let anyone cross it. It's nice to be nice but it's foolish to be walked over.

I don't think the Ozturk family knew what they were quite letting themselves in for when they thought it would be a good idea for Denny and I to work together, but whatever the thought I think they had to have a rethink as once I'd settled down me and Denny quickly got into our old ways. It was not going to be easy to separate us as we began our drunken binges where we would simply disappear for the afternoon and a search party would be sent out looking for us. Me and the bonny lad were one step ahead and had already sussed out all the bars in Armutalan and had our very own little room in the back of Musti's where we could quietly have a game of darts and a pint and mock our bosses as they would frantically drive around looking for us. We were a nightmare when we worked apart in the old days so imagine what damage we could do when we worked together. Try as they might, they couldn't stop our drunken binges but one night they decided enough was enough and when Denny went to the bar and asked Ali the waiter for a pint he was refused as the bosses had limited him to only a couple of pints a night. Denny, being the stubborn bastard he is, went to Ihsan and asked him for 10 lira which he then took to the market next door, bought a bottle of brandy, went back into Sera Beach sat at the bar and drank the lot. Jesus when I think what we were drinking then it was no wonder we used to suggest to each other that it is a possibility that we might not live the season out. In an act of desperation Ihlan the owner of Sera Beach granted me and Denny one day off together on the promise that we would behave for the rest of the week to which we agreed. That lasted about two weeks! I didn't work during the day so spent most of it lazing around the Club Sera swimming pool chatting with guests and trying to get Gold shop customers. I was doing quite well and one particular morning Denny informed me he was going down to the bazaar as he felt a Pakistani couple who were guests at the Club Sera had been ripped off at a Jewellers down there. He was going to try and get them some money back as he felt they had been overcharged by a fiver! "A fiver Den, are you fucking insane?" İ asked him. "You're going all the way down the bazaar and arguing over a fiver?" But Denny wouldn't see sense and asked me to come along with him, foolishly I did… after the lady's husband told me he would buy me a couple of pints. So off we went on the Dolmuş. Now I'm no fan of the bazaar. İt's a dangerous place full of mafia types and when we arrived me and the fella sat and had a pint while Denny took the lady to the shop where she had bought this bracelet the previous day. One pint led to two, then three and by now I started to panic because Denny and the lady hadn't returned. İ told the bloke to stay there while I went to investigate. When I opened the shop door I heard the owner on the phone speaking Turkish and asking his friend for a gun. When I asked what was going on the guy angrily shouted, "Is this your friend, get him out of my shop before I kill him." I knew the guy was serious and began to barge Denny and the woman out of the back door of the shop but oh no Denny wasn't having none of it and was going nowhere until he got the fiver back! I literally had to push him out of the door and told him of the imminent danger. As we got outside I saw two men approaching and I grabbed hold of Denny and we ran until we reached the relative safety of the Attaturk Statue. We met the couple back at the Apartments and they just didn't have a clue as to what had just happened. But for sure if we hadn't run we would have both been in serious trouble that day, all over a bloody fiver. We were going to have some laughs that summer and Armutalan just didn't really know how to handle me and Denny, come to think about it, no-one did!

Denny was at his best that summer at Sera Beach, but one night he surpassed himself when everyone was calling him telling him that he had been on television back in the UK and that they had videoed it and would bring it across the next week, these were the days before social media. Sure enough the customer brought the video across and it was quite simply one of the funniest things I have ever seen.
So one of these undercover holiday watchdog type programmes had come to review the Club Sera and Denny was entrusted by the management to show them around. So this lady walks into the apartments rooms and immediately sees a cockroach walking across the floor and the lady asked "what is it, does it fly?" With this Denny booted it across the floor and exclaimed "It fucking does now pet."

The season was building up nicely and Sera Beach was busy. Denny was still doing his Tina Turner, Al Jolson and Belly Dance and I had an assistant to help me. That assistant went on to be a great friend of mine and he is now one of the best DJs I have ever heard. Although I would love to take some credit for that I can't as, the now relatively famous DJ Nimo, was a natural. I would go on to work with him in years to come. But he will one day make it big time and no-one would deserve it more, he's a class act.

Working on the beach compared to working at Omar Sharif's was like stepping up from the third division into the Premiership.

We had some characters in the restaurant as well as a couple of major league love rats. To be honest, at that point, I didn't really realise what a Love Rat was. In fact although love rats were obviously around at that time it wasn't of the epidemic proportion it is today. Yeah at Omar Sharif we had had Mico who would regularly receive gifts from girls in exchange for his promises of love and long nights of passion but it was harmless. Sure he broke many women's hearts but they would get over it in time. I also knew Turks who would sleep with older women for cash but again it wasn't hurting anyone. I knew of one guy, who's still around today, who advertised his name on his car window screen with the title 'sex therapist' underneath it. But no-one got hurt and even today if women want to go over to Turkey for sex, which a lot of them do, then what's the problem? But when I started work on the beach, I saw the more sadistic side of what damage these guys could cause and it's something that I feel needs urgently addressing as we see the number of women being stripped of all their assets soar to epidemic proportions. I will dedicate a full chapter to this later on but for now I'll just tell you I would sit and watch these guys operate and, as foolish as you may think these women are, please don't underestimate the powers of a love rat.

Full house at Sera Beach for the football

Myself and the one and only DJ Nimo

As if I ever needed encouragement from a drunken Denny

A rare night out on the Marina with Yunus
and his university friends

If I thought working at Omar Sharif's was an eye opener, then trust me, that first season at Sera beach was on another level and literally anything went and nothing shocked. I was propositioned a few times by elderly ladies wanting to pay me a hundred pounds to go with their friend. Although I like the older women my milf fantasies stop at forty years old and some of these women were old enough to be my grandmother! Alas because I didn't want to indulge that doesn't mean to say that my work colleagues wouldn't. Without mentioning his name, I always knew a young man who would enthusiastically oblige. Maybe on a good night we would have had twenty single women in Omar Sharif's to choose from. In Sera Beach there were a hundred, so for your average Turk it was heaven. I was choosy though and wasn't particularly there for good times with girls. I just loved the full package that a summer season in Turkey brought. But most important to me was the culture, my friends and that atmosphere.

I met many friends that first season at Sera Beach but one scouse family who were staying at the Club Sera particularly stick in my mind. It was whilst walking around the pool one day that I got the familiar smell of cannabis. Looking around I saw this scouse lad laid on his sunbed with a huge spliff in his hand. I went over to investigate and when he invited me up to his room for a smoke then It would only be rude of me to refuse. Once inside the room he showed me the huge amount of resin that he had smuggled up his arse, it was the size of a snooker ball! Needless to say for two weeks he was my best mate! For those two weeks I barely lifted my head off my sun bed.

On arriving to work one night I saw Octay laughing, now as much as I initially hated him, I was beginning to take a liking to him and enquired as to what he found amusing. He pointed over to the scouser who was handing around a joint to all the staff and that was it, chaos. Wrong orders everywhere, wrong drinks, food wasn't arriving, in fact everywhere I went including the kitchen it was bedlam. I had to ask scouse to politely refrain from smoking in there anymore as the grief I was getting from customers was relentless.

I'm not going to go into detail about that particular season as it was like any other. İt was, however, going to be shortened as I got a telegram from Andrea in Holland telling me she was coming for a holiday with the full intention of taking me back to Holland with her. To be honest I was making no money as the season was exceptionally quiet and I remember it as if it was yesterday. I sat on the roadside in Armutalan without a penny in my pocket and I cried like a baby. Andrea arrived a week later and seeing the state I was in had nothing on her mind except getting me a ticket on the same flight as her. That never happened but she did indeed buy me a ticket and I would be flying to Holland by myself the day after her. First I had to inform my bosses of my intentions. They were far from happy, indeed on seeing my ticket Ihsan tried to snatch it off me and rip it up. We had a couple of Dutch guests who were going back to Eindhoven on the same flight as myself so I decided I would look after them for my final few days in the hope they would chaperone me on my flight home and that they did. But as if I could leave Marmaris without something happening and that morning was no different and we had only been traveling ten minutes! As most of you know there is a long incline up the road out of Marmaris that takes you past a spot where I used to sit and drink with the boys on a night as the sights overlooking İçmeler are stunning. İt was at the top of that hill that disaster struck. The Turkish driver hadn't shut the luggage door properly and as we took a sharp bend all the cases flew out and the flash of vinyl cases proceeded to skim the road and fly off the end of the cliff. My trusty old leather case never skimmed the road but hit the road and stuck to the hot road like glue. What could we do? Nothing! And despite them arguing with the driver that something needed to be done, much to my amusement, he just shrugged his shoulders and carried on!

7

Holland, Home From Home

I was met at Eindhoven airport by Andrea and I really didn't know what to expect. I loved Holland and after settling in I needed a job. At the time it wasn't difficult to find work and I ended up in a metal factory. A far cry from Marmaris İ know but Turkey never seemed far away as Holland has nearly half a million Turks living there. İt was inevitable that I would find a lot of my colleagues were Turks and to be honest it felt like home from home. The Netherlands have a policy at work that says you must try and speak Dutch in the workplace but to everyone's amusement I found my only way of communication was Turkish and the Turks took to me under their wing. İt was that first week when my boss pulled me aside with a smile on his face and politely asked me what an English man in Holland was doing speaking Turkish! A few months later I was to become the mediator in disagreements between Turks and the Dutch. İn a strange way the Dutch dislike the Turks who live there but they visit Turkey in their millions for holidays. They just can't tolerate them in their own country. Seems a little odd to me but believe me when I say these Turks who have settled in Europe, although keeping many of the traits of their native land, are hard work and a totally different kettle of fish indeed. Later on I was to see for myself how difficult it is for European Turks to settle back in Turkey and work in the tourism industry.

I loved my time at that metal factory although I was often caught in the middle of disagreement. One Christmas especially there was a huge argument going on. This was because the Christmas Hampers from our bosses contained alcohol and ham which the Muslims amongst the workforce found offensive. As far as I was concerned they didn't have a leg to stand on. I found it highly hypocritical as they don't celebrate Christmas and they were trying to dictate to us what we could have in our hampers. To me the simple answer would be to just take the bottle of wine and pork products out of the hamper themselves instead of us all suffering. But that wasn't good enough for them and I couldn't make them see sense. Subsequently we all got an alcohol and ham free hamper. In my opinion it was the Dutch who lost out simply because they pandered to every whim of the Turks and the Moroccans. For that I can only blame the Dutch.

A couple of years down the line I learned Dutch and the Turks looked on me as some sort of traitor as I mingled in with my Dutch colleagues. I was totally outcast by them simply because I ate during ramadam!

Although it would be a few years later when I returned to Marmaris as a worker, my now wife and I went every year for a holiday. This inevitably led me to spending more time with my friends there than my new wife. Although Andrea didn't like it, I'm afraid that's how it was. Marmaris was my second home and for one week only I had chance to catch up with old friends, including my old pal Denny.

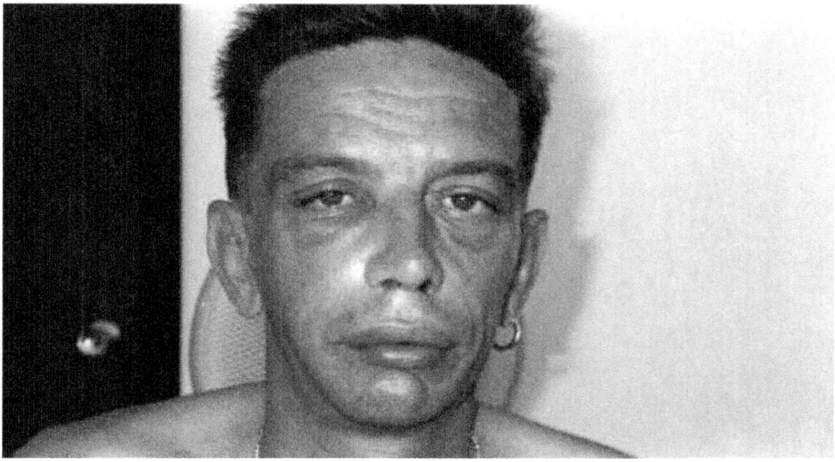

When things go wrong in Turkey. I lost two things that night in Amutulan, my pride and my teeth

My stag night in Tilburg

Myself, Dennis, Doug and Gav. On the train through Germany to watch England

On stage in Holland

It was my first ever holiday in Marmaris that saw me getting into one of the most frightening experiences of my life and it went like this. We were stopping at a hotel in Armutalan and our second day saw us have breakfast at the hotel's restaurant, it was poor. Needless to say we gave the place a miss over the next couple of days. Thinking we were ordinary holidaymakers they would curse us for not eating in their restaurant. Then after a evening out on the beach Andrea and I decided to have a night cap before bed. Unbeknown to us we were about to embark on a night that would see all hell break loose and I needed to call upon my friends at River Jewellery again!

We got seated in the bar area when the owner of the bar/hotel came over to us and asked why we never ate in his establishment. I said about the breakfast we had a few days prior and he didn't like it. His partner was a Dutch guy from the same town as us in the Netherlands and my wife actually knew his family. She got talking to him and they went on a trip down memory lane and she disclosed many personal details that would come back to haunt us later on. Admittedly I was drunk but I was on holiday. I'd had enough of the Dutch bloke telling me all about his experiences in Turkey and kindly asked the guy to leave our table as he was offending the Turks and knew nothing about my previous years working there. When I stood up to go to the bar I felt a blow to my face from behind and both the owner and his partner attacked me. I was repeatedly kicked and punched in my face while I lay helplessly on the floor. Customers and my wife looked on helplessly in horror. After the beating, that seemed to go on forever, I was left with a barely recognisable face and needed to get to the hospital as most of my teeth had been kicked out (see photo). I will make this quite clear now that I would never have gone to the police but facing a huge medical bill I would have to inform the police so to enable me to claim off my travel insurance. We spent the full night in hospital and they were actually blaming me for being drunk! I think we got out of the hospital as the morning sun came up and we had another dilemma, how the hell would we get to our apartment for our belongings as our room was just behind the restaurant. Luckily we managed to get our stuff unnoticed and proceeded to go to my ex boss's apartments just around the corner. So there we were, stood at the pool bar at 7am in the morning. I was stood there rubbing rakki on my gums when the Turkish partner from the night before walked in. He was angry and had been looking for me all night. He screamed at me why I had informed the police. Denny, who was stood next to me, disappeared. So it was me and my wife and this huge extremely pissed off Turk. I was scared and my wife was hysterical as he went on to tell me I would never leave Turkey alive. I had had enough and wasn't going to be intimidated. İ proceeded to inform him that I was no ordinary holidaymaker and in a desperate attempt to get rid of him I told him in no uncertain terms that if he wanted trouble then he had bitten off more than he could chew. İ immediately called Mikail who was sleeping, but within fifteen minutes, probably the longest fifteen minutes of my life, Mikail appeared with the police chief. As quickly as he appeared, the Turk disappeared. But that wasn't going to be the last of it as he put word out that Andrea's family back in Holland would pay the price for this and that I would be met by his Dutch/Turkish friends when we eventually got back to Holland.

The following days saw everyone asking me what had happened as my face was like something out of the Elephant man. What could I tell them but the truth and I although I won't mention the apartments where this attack took place, over the next few days I think the Turkish partner wished he had never laid eyes on me. His restaurant was closed down due to 'rats in his kitchen' and he received threats from every corner of Marmaris. So much so that I had to stop this as it would make matters worse for us when we got back to Holland. Andrea and I laid low for the rest of our holiday. I wanted no more repercussions. However, I was informed by many of my Turkish/Kurdish friends that as soon as we were on the plane back to Holland then this issue would be properly sorted and indeed it was, Turkish style. I was given a number of a renowned Kurdish family living in Holland and was told that should there be any repercussions to call them, they would watch over us until it all died down.

Settling down in Holland was difficult. Especially March/April time when I started getting itchy feet for the start of the season. Denny didn't help by repeatedly calling me telling me to come over for the season. But I managed it, although I still think If it wasn't for my Turkish friends in Holland I wouldn't have lasted the six years I did not returning for the summer season. I was trying to lead a normal life and reluctantly I resisted all attempts to get me back over there. I later went on to buy my own house in Holland and although I had an excellent new job, I still secretly yearned for Marmaris. I still used to hear from Sevil. She called me once out of the blue while I was at a friend's wedding in Germany. She asked if I would go to Istanbul and marry her. My feelings for Sevil never died but, as tempted as I was, I just knew deep down what a mountain to climb that would be and realistically speaking, as much as I wanted her, the negatives far outweighed the positives. I just had to get my head down and try and cherish the memories we had together.

8

The Rat Trap

And so to the chapter I have been dreading… why? Well in a nutshell, Turkish romances are a very sensitive and controversial subject where I'm going to walk through a minefield of eggshells. In doing so I am sure I will receive a barrage of hate from every angle. But as with everything I've written in this book I can only write from experience and what I've seen firsthand. My apologies in advance if it upsets you but save your breath with any hostile comments, I've heard it all before!

Statistics show that seventy five percent of single ladies who holiday in Turkish resorts will enjoy their holidays with no issues and would probably go back. However this chapter is about the remaining twenty five percent, the twenty five percent that find a holiday romance. Of those twenty five percent probably five percent will go on to form a meaningful and long term relationship which often involves marriage and children.

Sometimes the truth is a bitter pill to swallow and if involved in any way I sincerely hope it works out for you and that you get to become one of those rare ladies in the five percent club.

I would also like to point out that the game has changed in recent years as there is now a minimum wage for resort workers in Turkey unlike before when they were paid on a commission only basis. This is why back then the hassle from restaurants was far worse. The whole love rat syndrome was at epidemic proportions before the minimum wage was introduced. Indeed, there used to be a Facebook group called "Turkish Love Rats" dedicated to the subject and it was brutal as ladies got into bitter arguments as to "who was the girlfriend of Mehmet from the Turtle bar". Sometimes a dozen ladies laid claim to Mehmet. As an outsider looking in it was edge of your seat drama, however for the ladies involved it was truly heart breaking.

Now I'm not going to label Turks who sleep with many different ladies a season "Love Rats" it's more "Lover boys" as breaking a ladies heart is small scale compared to the more cunning and ruthless love rats who would take, not just a woman's heart but also her money at the blink of an eye and they don't give a flying fuck who they hurt along the way. These guys go against everything Islam stands for and labelling them rats is an insult to rodents.

Over the years I have seen the way these guys work hundreds of times. It was something I never got involved with though, apart from once in the early days of my time in Marmaris and it got me into a shit load of trouble! There is nothing a rat hates more than someone interfering and disrupting their evil and twisted intentions. It's very dangerous to get involved because a woman can also turn on you as they have been brainwashed into thinking their relationship is special.

Ladies I mean no disrespect when I say this but anyone can find a Turkish boyfriend in a resort whether your not the slimmest, prettiest, youngest or the richest. You can find anybody who would give you a night of passion, however younger lover boys do go for the more prettier girls, love rats don't discriminate and can smell vulnerability from a mile away and unfortunately particularly vulnerable ladies are who they prey on.

One thing I never grasped is why these ladies walk hand in hand with their lover boys parading them around like some sort of trophy. Inevitably a few days later they got a bite on the bum that's more painful than any mosquito bite and their bragging rights quickly turn to one of heartbreak, embarrassment, and shame!

My first restaurant Omar Sharif didn't really have any rats at the time. We did however have one lover boy who was an expert in the art and he was good, real good. His name was Micho, a tall handsome Turk from Ankara who had just come out of his military service. His English was perfect and his ability to pull the women was a joy to watch. That first season I worked with him we became really good friends. When we closed the restaurant at night we would take our customers on a bar crawl down Bar Street. Obviously we both got free drinks plus the commission from thirty odd of our customers spends, which was pretty lucrative, but our customers loved it! Although they thought we were taking them to the best bars we were actually taking them to bars who would pay us the best commission. In those days it was usually B52. Micho was our head waiter and was, like all our staff back then, solely committed to making our restaurant the best in the area and that we did! He was probably the best waiter I have ever worked with.

With regards to the ladies, it was very rare he didn't have a girl to take home on a night. Taking a lady "home" though was not really an option as staff quarters were not ideal, if you have ever seen the places resort workers sleep you will understand why. For those who don't know what staff accommodations are like, they are all packed in like sardines. I say they because fortunately I was never expected to sleep in staff quarters. I was blessed, I had proved more than my worth so was given a lovely room in the attic of the hotel opposite and it was heaven. Although being within fifty yards of our restaurant meant the boss often sent the lads across to get me if we had an issue; this occurred all to often. It was also beneficial to me though as it was a place where Sevil could come. She used the guise of being a Turkish guest and booked a room near mine and then sneaked to my room when all was quiet.

So with staff quarters being a no no to take the ladies the Romeos took them to a hotel around the corner that became the go-to place for waiters wanting a night of passion. It was called The Star Otel and is still open today. Back then it was strictly not allowed for Turks to stay in hotels, this place was one of maybe three across Marmaris that allowed it. It was, for want of a better word "A knocking shop"! Every night it was full of Turks and their conquests. However there was a twist at this place and everyone used this blag. The Hotel was only a tenner a night but the lady friends were told that the hotel costs forty pounds but he would go halves. So after happily handing over her twenty pounds he would pay a tenner to the receptionist and put a tenner in his back pocket. Not a bad earner if they were doing this seven nights a week, he was getting his leg over, had a nice comfy bed to sleep in and made a tidy profit to boot. Ingenious!… and every Turk was onto it.

So I'm going to begin by taking you back to 1998, my first season working as a hassle man, a time when every resort worker worked on a commission basis. It was my job to bring the customers into our restaurant. As I've previously explained it wasn't difficult for me. For myself and for Denny, Tuesdays and Thursday were "white chicken days". It was our name for new customers and they were huge days for us as they were Airtours transfer days. A great chance to hassle white chickens. They stood out like a sore thumb, brilliant white and wondering about aimlessly as they tried to find their bearings. Now getting these white chickens in on their first day was extremely important as it usually meant they would spend a lot of their holiday in our restaurant. When I caught some white chickens all the staffs' attention turned to them. For a hassle man then a family of eight or more was like hitting the jackpot for the restaurant as it meant money. Even if they came in just a few times during their holiday it was extremely profitable. There was one thing I never understood about the Turks though, if a family that had frequented our restaurant didn't come in one night then my boss would be crazy as to why? As much as I tried to explain to him that British people like to try different places, he was not having any of it and blamed either the service or the staff. It came to a point where he would send the twins out on their bicycles looking for the said family! That may seem extreme but as I'm sure you are aware, should you go AWOL one night from your favourite restaurant they want to know where you have been as if they actually think they have a god-given right to know why you would go anywhere else! However should you go into a rival's restaurant then all hell breaks loose and they blame the rivals for stealing their white chickens…again I would put this down to jealousy and Turkish pride.

Now a family of white chickens walking up to my restaurant meant I had a free hand to give them anything they wanted. The more of them there were the better it was as I could offer free meals, free drinks, basically free anything on their first day. That still applies today, so if you go on holiday with a large group of family or friends then you have massive bargaining power… use it! You will find the hassle man will give you absolutely anything to get you in. The first things you need to be asking them is do kids eat free or how many free drinks are they going to give you. Try it, you will save yourselves a lot of money in the long run. I can assure you it works every time.

Now those families of white chickens were extremely important to my boss as they brought huge financial reward for the restaurant. But for the staff, the biggest jackpot was a group of white hens. You could see the delight in their eyes if I managed to catch a group of ladies and brought them into our place. The waiters were all over them like flies, claiming bragging rights to each individual lady, even if the ladies didn't show the slightest bit of interest. Micho was the man charged with charming the ladies and he did a great job. Should one of our staff manage to actually attract one of the ladies then it was more than likely that they would all come in every night to appease their friend who had fallen head over heels with their lover boy.

Sometimes however the ladies were not appealing to any of the staff, that is when the boss stepped in and encouraged the staff to take one for the team. Although they weren't happy about it someone had to make a move on one of the ladies so that they would come in every night. When nobody volunteered my boss would rely on a young waiter of ours called Ozzy who, whilst he wasn't your normal outgoing handsome Turk, would do anything to climb the ladder of hierarchy. More about Ozzy later as a few years on our young, shy little waiter would turn into a love rat himself!

There was another group of people who were always a welcome sight… previous customers of ours. When they walked up towards our place we just knew they were coming in and we made a big fuss of them. Well I say "we" but to be honest I have the memory of a goldfish but these Turks have this uncanny skill to recognise anybody. Believe me, if these people came into our restaurant ten years ago our staff would remember them! They all can do it! It left me in a very precarious situation when all the staff were welcoming them with open arms, the customers obviously knew me because they came to me shouting my name but I'm thinking, "Please give me a clue because as far as I'm concerned I've never seen you before in my life." This happened to me later on when I worked in Bacchus. I was living in Holland and married, we struck up a friendship with a couple from a small town outside of Tilburg where we lived. We had visited them and indeed stayed over a couple of times at their home the winter before and this particular season they had been all over Marmaris looking for me. They were turning up to surprise me and surprise me they did! Although we were having group hugs I'm looking puzzledly at Denny who didn't help matters by saying, "Don't you know who they are?" Enjoying my embarrassment Denny kept on going on, so I whispered to Denny "For fuck sake Den who are they?" I did remember them when prompted but that couple of minutes where I didn't, felt like a lifetime!

The reason behind these first couple of paragraphs is I just want to give you an insight into the thinking of a restaurant's staff. Customers are a commodity and we would stoop to anything to keep our white chickens as regular customers. We have just over six months to make as much money as possible… And of course the Turks welcome you as friends, it's lovely to see old customers relishing in the fact that we remembered them. For me however, the truth is, in all my years, I could count on two hands the actual customers who have stayed in my memory. And, apart from Sevil obviously, probably one lady!

It was strictly business for me as it was for all our staff at Omar's, that's what made us so successful. That wasn't to say each one of our customers wasn't special, they were and we always tried to give them a holiday to remember.

So what is it that makes us leave our brains at Dalaman? I think holidaymakers who travel to any foreign resort do. It's just what we do. We are relaxed, it's all new and exciting and we can get drunk, that's normal! But when you throw in a few thousand Turkish resort workers with their charm, good looks and their attentive manner then it's a game changer that makes Turkey what it is. It kind of makes us feel special and good about ourselves and why not? You're on holiday and looking good so it's nice to feel special and attractive and that someone actually appreciates the money you've spent preparing for your holiday.

So let's break this love rat thing down. Unfortunately the norm is the older you get the pounds etc. start to show and you fall into another category but for the young girls; I can break them down into two categories. The latter of the two I have a lot of sympathy for but the first deserve most of what they get. We got many in Omar Sharif's but when I moved to work on the beach it was embarrassing to see British girls sometimes.

You know if a Turk lays claim to a girl and that said girl went sleeping with other blokes from different bars/restaurants then that Turkish pride raises it's head. I've seen hundreds of fights caused by British girls bringing their UK mentality with them that makes them think they can sleep with anyone they want. Well this is

Turkey and it simply can't be done without reprisals and they can get be pretty damn serious.

I think we all have seen these girls with their backsides and boobs hanging out staggering down the street, bottle in hand shouting obscenities at every Turk who dares lay eyes on them until they see one who takes their fancy. Then it's a quickie back scuttle on the beach or a knee trembler down a dark passage. Basically these girls who wouldn't get a second glance back home become the centre of attention for any hot blooded Turk and boy do they make the most of it! I saw many and still do and it makes me ashamed to be British, where is their dignity?

So let's look at it from a Turk's point of view. As most of you know, resort workers travel from all over Turkey to work the summer season. In winter time these resorts are very quiet and you would barely recognise them during the closed season. But come April the workers will travel miles to come and work in these resorts. They come from far and wide but mostly from the east of Turkey. This means a bus journey of up to twenty four hours! A lot of these guys come from small villages where there is very little work, little money and little if no chance of sex. As secular and westernised a country as Turkey has become being Islamic in Turkey means that no worthy Muslim girl will give up her virginity until her wedding day. Therefore there is an hormonal uproar for a young man as he goes through his adolescent years without being able to satisfy his natural urges. Looking back at my younger years when I went through the stages of experimenting with sex I can't comprehend how any young Muslim male copes.

However the need for money and work has families sending their sons to work in one of Turkey's holiday resorts. It is often a family's only source of income, so come April the lads take a small bag of clothes and head off for the summer season. You can imagine the feelings that greet them when they arrive in their chosen resorts and it's full of topless ladies on the beach and drunken scantily dressed British girls looking for a night of fun and not being afraid to eagerly offer themselves up for it! These guys will have heard the stories about how crazy British girls can be between the sheets which is something they are not used to. It is understood that most Muslim women don't usually indulge in unconventional sex. It's simply not on the agenda (however I will add that sex with Sevil although conventional was probably the best and most passionate I've ever had). So for a Turkish resort worker to experience a European's idea of sex is something of an eye opener. I often heard the lads bragging about how many times they actually had performed intercourse the night before and I have no doubt about their stamina. For little old me though, who could manage it twice if I was lucky, I had the advantage of performing oral sex, something that most Muslim men find dirty and something they just can get their head around, pardon the pun!

These days of cheap holidays, huge Universal Credit pay-outs etc. Turkey has attracted cheap customers wanting a champagne holiday on lemonade money, the type of girls who will get pissed on a cheap bottle of vodka in their apartments and then head out on to the beach feeling like super models because they are getting attention of hot-blooded Turks. But reading what I've just written, it's not difficult to pull a fella in a Turkish resort is it? Anyone with a pulse can find a Turk only willing to oblige in the dirty deed. I suppose, as Brits, these girls stand out like a sore thumb because, to us, just looking at these girls you know they are going to be trouble and when they open their potty mouths it just confirms it. Unfortunately the Turks don't see that and with their penis controlling their heads any game is fair game! It's these girls who hassle the Turks not the other way around and should one of them form a relationship with a resort worker and it all goes pear shaped the girls can turn nasty and I mean real nasty and can make life quite difficult for the restaurant/bar as the girls don't just take their rejection out on the guy but will also stop at nothing at giving the restaurant a bad name on every Facebook page they can find.

The next type of young lady I have a lot of empathy for. I have met many and although I learned never to get involved, in my first season It was difficult to watch these girls falling in love with a Turkish waiter. It's like you're watching a car crash waiting to happen but there is nothing you can do about it. They simply won't listen so it's simply not worth trying "Their" Turkish boyfriend is different to the rest. Oh I wish I had a thousand Lira for every time I had heard that!

Gullible, naïve and silly are just a few labels these girls get and, although I agree they have a bit of all the above, they also have a beautiful soul that makes them vulnerable. I've witnessed the strongest and the most independent girls fall for Turkish romances and can't understand why?

These girls are often educated and from good families and obviously, as most ladies do, they know the reputation that Turkish resorts have. Still they fall for it though or should I say fall into it as this is not something a young lady had even considered when they booked a holiday to a Turkish holiday resort. They would probably find any suggestion that they may fall in love with a Turkish waiter as laughable, but they do though albeit not intentionally. Without getting involved I have spoken to hundreds of these girls over the years and what I have found is that they have one trait that affects them all, they are obstinate! Once these girls get hooked they are all in and will not listen to anyone, you probably know of a friend who has been through it and appreciate just how difficult it is to offer advice to someone who doesn't want to listen. Push the agenda and she will quickly become an ex friend as anything they see as an obstacle to their Turkish romance will be brushed aside!

As I've previously mentioned, approximately twenty five percent of ladies holidaying in a Turkish resort will have a holiday romance with a Turk/Kurd with maybe five percent who are lucky enough to make it a long term or permanent relationship. But what's so special about that tiny minority of five percent that last? I know lots of them and they will be the first to tell you to make a relationship work with a Turk then it's a challenge of monumental proportions. So what's the secret? How do the twenty five percent get dwindled down to those brave ladies who make the five percent club?

Well, generally, it starts like this. They go on holiday with friends/family meet a Turkish resort worker and then go back on their own. This is where it all starts. Turkish resort workers have to put quite a bit of work into a lady coming on holiday who hasn't particularly come for romance, however once hooked these ladies become part of the twenty-five percenters. They will have been charmed to the point of no return. These ladies have probably got a dull, mundane life in the UK and have probably had a bad experience or relationship with some dickhead who has made her want to forget long term relationships for a while. They go to Turkey and find someone who treats them with respect, dignity and makes her feel like maybe there is hope after all. She just needs convincing and if anyone can convince her a Turkish lover boy can! So for the sake of me going through the whole scenario I will refer to the resort worker as Mehmet and this scenario is played out a thousand times every week in all Turkish holiday resorts.

You are on holiday with friends and get drawn to this young, handsome waiter who is giving you the eye. Whilst other ladies have eyes for him, he seems to be paying particular attention to you, he makes you feel attractive, wanted and very special. You are now on Mehmet's radar. He will sit and talk to you when it gets quiet and you will feel flattered that he's spending time with you when he could have anyone. He will, for the duration of your holiday, treat you like a princess, the way you have been craving to be treated. Whether you have sex or just a kiss and a cuddle depends on how he feels for you but one thing is for sure, when you get on the aeroplane home you will not be able to get him out of your mind! You will both have probably made plans that you will return alone and sure enough on your return to the UK the first thing you do is book a holiday back alone!

Congratulations, you have just joined the twenty-five percent club and once you have taken that first step up the ladder there is little chance of you turning back without heartache. Or worse, you will climb further up the ladder and encounter the many pitfalls it involves. Both you and Mehmet will have discussed the "future" whilst on that first holiday and probably declared your undying love for each other but once back to UK and making plans to return to see Mehmet alone you will come up against your first barrier… friends and family, they will think you have simply lost your mind. Looking from the outside you can't really blame them.

I'm pretty sure that what you expect on your return to Turkey alone and what actually happens are two different things. You don't know it yet but Turkish culture means you will never be the most important lady in his life. His mother is and always will be and that's something that will never change. So to please his mum and his family Mehmet has to work hard and send money home. Therefore his job will become paramount before you, before anyone. You will always play second fiddle to his only way of making money, his job and his boss.

So here you are on holiday alone and you will get a small insight into a resort worker's life. You will find yourself alone with nothing to do accept lay on Mehmet's beach or sit in his restaurant wanting his attention. But I'm afraid apart from his three hours break in the afternoon and the time whilst his restaurant is closed, you're not going to get a great deal of YOU time!

I had a few ladies come to see me when I worked in Marmaris, it's a delicate juggling act and one I didn't relish as my break times and my sleep were important for me. When I had a "girlfriend" visit me, after those first couple of nights of passion, it was a long drawn-out haul which had me counting the days to when they would actually return home.

Another thing that you will quickly realise is that your holiday money you've worked so hard for isn't going to go far because Mehmet isn't going to have a great deal of money. Although many people think that the resort workers maybe are a little shy when it comes to spending their hard-earned money the truth of the matter is that they are Islamic and every penny they earn will be going home to their family. It's difficult to get your head around but again you better get used to it because this is how it will always be, family come first. I would point out at this stage that he may ask you to bring him some gifts from the UK and for some strange reason you will feel obliged to take him a pair of trainers or a bottle of whisky across. Please leave it at just that. Should he ask for things you simply can't afford or indeed asks you for cash whilst your over there this is your first warning sign you may have a "Love Rat" on your hands. This is especially so if he uses the old excuse of family members in hospital amongst other excuses for money. You should stop this sort of relationship there and then! You probably won't and that may lead you down a very expensive slippery path. In Turkey sometimes your heart rules your head but I would urge you to follow your instincts as this will save you a hell a lot of heartache. I've seen many a lady sat there in my restaurant alone and I've also heard the waiters talking about these girls in Turkish and laughing at them for being so gullible. It hurt to hear it but again I wasn't going to get involved. I would however often talk with these girls and they would openly talk to me about the plans she had with her Turkish partner, how they would get married, have a future together and live happily ever after, the truth being in most circumstances that in winter time she would return to the UK and he would return to his village and apart from the odd facetime that's as far as it was going to go. I repeat trust your instincts, should you feel Mehmet and his work colleagues are talking about you and laughing it's not a good sign. Even today I will not sit in the company of my Turkish friends and my wife and speak Turkish. It's a mark of respect, I just wouldn't dream of speaking Turkish while sat with my wife. My friends all know this and respect it.

Another misconception is that ladies think just because Mehmet's work colleagues tell you that "Mehmet is not normally one to fall in love so quickly" then it's probably bullshit and they have been told to tell you that. I'm afraid to say I've backed my colleagues up with this old chestnut many times knowing full well my colleague had "fallen in love" a dozen times that season.

Another sign that should set alarm bells ringing is when you tell Mehmet when you plan to come over to visit him and he makes excuses that he won't be there because he has to go home for what could be a variety of reasons. Then he will go on to suggest a more suitable time. The truth is he most probably will be there but will have to juggle his calendar as this may clash with another lady visiting him. A resort worker has a calendar and must at all costs avoid two ladies visiting him at the same time, he will find any excuse.

I remember at Sera beach when I had a lady calling the restaurant a dozen times a day asking for me and I really didn't have the guts to tell her I didn't want her to come. My boss at the time was getting pretty fed up with it and got into a heated argument with me so I said to him to just make an excuse for me please. After thinking I was in the clear having not heard anything for a couple of days I got calls from my friends back in the UK worried about my wellbeing. I asked my boss what he had told the girl and he said that he had told her I had an accident on my moped and had sadly died! Of course the girl had contacted one of my close friends and word quickly spread to my family back home who were naturally worried sick!

So your holiday's over and it's time to say goodbye again. You will probably go home and work your backside off for one more chance to see Mehmet before the season's over. At this point you actually believe you have a relationship and try convincing your friends and family back home that you have. Don't expect them to be over the moon for you, they are cautious, concerned and genuinely worried where this may lead, understandably so, as from an outsider looking in you're crazy for even considering a long distance relationship with a Turk. But you won't listen, in fact quite the opposite, in your mind this relationship is special and no-one, but no-one, is going to tell you otherwise. Should anyone try and shatter your dreams then you will simply push them away.

In most cases these relationships will fizzle out after a season for various reasons. Either you cannot finance these holidays anymore, you have discovered he's been cheating or simply you have met someone in the UK. Out of these scenarios finding out he's been cheating is probably the worse as you are going to have everyone telling you they "told you so". Unfortunately you're just going to have to take it on the chin. Most don't however and it can take a long time to get over. Some ladies however, actually go back to Turkey in search of another Turkish romance and it starts all over again.

I have given you a few warning signs here but the truth is although you might see these signs, you don't want to see them or listen to the obvious because as a twenty five percenter you aspire to be one thing, part of the elite five percent club. Truth be told this is only the start of the journey though and you have a lot of blood, sweat and tears before becoming part of this rare breed.

Another major thing you must take into consideration, and it is important, and that's where they are from. People will tell you Turkey is a secular country and indeed it is, in theory. But, especially these days, there are modern liberal Turks who live in the metropolitan towns and Cities. They are not practicing Muslims and have a very modern way of living their life. Take Bodrum for example, when you see the Turks holiday there you wouldn't know you were in an Islamic country. Izmir, where I have had the pleasure to visit a few times, is a thriving metropolitan City and those famous Izmir ladies have worn short skirts and heels since I first visited in 1998. Wow I will never forget my first visit! Not only was it the best street kebab I've ever had (for 20p!), I have never seen so many stunningly beautiful girls. I have a lot of modern friends, friends that have a modern outlook, who want to do things we do in the west but although they are modern in their thinking, they are Islamic and although some sail close to the wind as liberal as they are they are still Muslim and abide by most things the Koran teaches them.

And then you have the Turks who live in the villages where most lean towards being practicing Muslims. The villages are usually where these generations have lived for years. Some still herd cattle and live like their elders did. The villages have traditions to uphold and most of the inhabitants are strict Muslims. They practice the old-fashioned values. Life for the people in these small villages, particularly in the east of Turkey, are tough with little work and poor housing. But they have their families and their faith and for them that is the meaning of life. I have many practicing Muslim friends and although they lose their way in the bright lights of the resorts they return back to their villages in winter and get back on track with their faith.

For me I respect both, to me religion is not important which is why I never converted for Sevil. I'm not a hypocrite and wouldn't convert just because it would have suited my agenda. Whilst living in Holland I saw the third generation of Turks trying to juggle Western thinking and their Turkish roots. I felt for them and always knew which bar to find my Muslim friends during Ramadam… in the Irish Bar where none of their fellow Muslims would see them.

I guess what I'm saying here is, if you have found yourself a modern Turk then it's going to be a lot easier than if they are practicing Muslims living in small villages. As a westerner you could walk about in Izmir and would be largely unnoticed. However if you walked around a village in the east of Turkey you are going to stand out like a sore thumb. Of course with western views comes western habits and although any Turkish household would welcome you in as a friend a more traditional Turkish village would find it difficult to accept your western ways, they have a lot of the traditions that need to be respected. When you have the honour of being invited into a more Islamic village where money is tight, as daunting as it can be for any Westerner including myself, it is a joy to treasure and although you may not appreciate it at the time, I can assure you, not only do you get to see the old, traditional Turkey but as a guest they will make it as special as humanly possible for you.

So how do ladies make the five percent club? Well one thing's for sure you will need money. I've seen many ladies think it's as simple as moving over to Turkey to spend time with their boyfriends. For that you will need two things a job and a place to live. Apart from being a poorly paid rep then I'm afraid there are very few job opportunities around where you will not require a work visa and they are extremely rare things to obtain. Without a work visa then you can't work full stop. The days of going to Rhodes to renew your visa are well gone and the rules for your three months stay have all changed these days, you can't just leave the country these days and come back to a further three months, those three months are now divided into a year so it doesn't matter how many times you leave the country you are still only entitled to a three months stay and if you go over this you will land yourself with a huge fine and a chance of being deported and landed with a total ban of visiting Turkey for a very long time (it used to be six years). You will also need somewhere to live which with today's economy will prove very expensive as property prices have skyrocketed in Turkey. So the question is how will you subsidise an apartment without a well paid job. The answer will probably be that you have savings but believe me without a meaningful job then your savings will quickly dwindle in one summer season. I know many people who go over to Turkey for the summer with a five-figure sum and live like a tourist and their money is gone by the end of the season, subsequently they go home with nothing but a drink habit.

They say money makes the world go around but having money for certain ladies can make them very vulnerable in Turkish resorts because love rats smell money like a shark smells blood. These ladies tend to be aged between thirty and sometimes in their sixties. Now I can look at ladies and know they've got a few bob just by their demeanor, the way they dress and the amount of jewellery that adorns their body. These ladies are quiet often introverts and are quite happy to keep themselves to themselves but what they don't show is their vulnerability… until you dig a little deeper. A love rat's victims are all of the above. For the average man they might not stand out but for a love rat they stand out a mile. The ladies don't know it yet but within a fifteen minute evaluation process a love rat can spot a potential victim's vulnerabilities. These ladies may be divorced, widowed or simply have suffered a trauma that has taken away their self confidence, this makes them cannon fodder for the seasoned love rat. Once evaluated the love rat will decide if this lady is worth investing his time in and if he feels she is, he will spend as much time as needed to hook his victim, they are in no hurry, this is an investment and he needs to treat it as such. Your average love rat will be in his thirties/forties. Believe me once they have ladies hooked they will stop at nothing to reel them in and unlike lover boys, the rats will take it slow, they may initially invest money by taking you out for meals etc. and they will undoubtedly make you feel like the woman you haven't felt for many years. They won't try to get you into bed immediately, they won't tell you they love you on the first date and they definitely will tell you everything you want to hear about both yourself and themselves. Most of it will be lies but they play this game every season and will answer every question you have in your mind about why he would want to be with you, it's like shelling peas to them. Now they may profess to be everything they are not but without a doubt the ladies lack of confidence will find her asking herself what does he see in me?

You know in the first chapter in this book when I first laid eyes on Sevil, I asked myself many times what does she see in me? She was beautiful, rich, confident. What did I bring to the table? I wasn't particularly handsome and I definitely wasn't rich so you may ask yourself how I knew I wasn't getting played though. Well that first season I worked as a barman, she knew I was skint but she was the one taking all the risks, she was married with a child, her husband was rich and she had a what appeared to be a beautiful life except she was missing one thing in life… love. And I was the one who was going to change all that. I on the other hand had nothing to lose, I suppose you could say like it was like a love rat scenario in reverse as it was me who had nothing and her who had it all but for a Turkish woman to fall in love with an English guy it was extremely dangerous and it was Sevil who was putting her whole life at stake for me. So when I asked the question 'why me' to myself, I knew one hundred percent it was for nothing but love! She never asked me for anything but love and I was in no position to give her anything but my love and this is how I knew it was real.

A love rat is clever, once he discovers a lady's vulnerabilities, he will play on them without her even realising it and before long she will fall into a trap that will prove very hard to get out of. The love rat knows how to reel ladies in and can play the long game if he feels it's going to pay big dividends. He will be patient, it could take months before the cracks start to appear and believe me they inevitably will. However this will be too late for his victim as he has led her to believe she is the love of his life and she is swept into some euphoric fairy-tale that will change her life forever. From the outside the lady's friends and family (most have children/grandkids) will try to make her see reality but the love rat has probably already pre warned her that she will face objection but to ignore them as it was only their love that matters. I've had many families contact me over the years with that very dilemma and my answer is always the same. "There is nothing you can do". The more anyone objects, the further the victim will push them away. Again as with the younger ladies the first warning sign will be asking for things however you've been evaluated so it's not just clothes, money or a bottle of whisky the rat will ask for, oh no, he hasn't invested all this time for little things like that, he wants only money, big money!

A visa to the UK used to be a love rats' main goal but as regulations get stricter in the UK and with word getting back to them that Britain isn't all it's cracked up to be, it's less fashionable to go for the passport anymore. The goal now appears to be their own restaurant or apartment in Turkey so they can live happily ever after. Again he will strike when he feels he has reeled his victim in but should he ask for money (for a variety of reasons) I would expect the victim to run a mile, the sad truth is they rarely do as it's way too late.

I have seen many restaurants in Turkey paid for by ladies. I know one in particular, still going today, that changed hands three times in one season for £30,000 a time, all to

British ladies! When the cracks appear it's too late, they can't go to the police or get a solicitor as they have only a three month holiday visa and no resident's permit. Therefore they haven't got a leg to stand on… and don't the Love Rats know it!

Going back to my days at Omar Sharif and, as I previously mentioned, our young waiter Ozzy! The year I was deported he met a holidaymaker called Cathy (named changed) who was twenty years his senior. I knew her well, she was glamorous, strong willed, educated and worked as an investment manager for a high street bank. When I returned in 2001 Ozzy had his own restaurant paid for by her and he eventually moved to England where he still resides today. He is now the owner of a string of kebab shops down south and, as with many Turks I know, came to the UK after meeting a holidaymaker, got a visa lived together until he obtained his indefinite leave to remain and buggered off leaving the lady with nothing but a broken heart and a shed load of debt.

But the women who fall for the love rats charm resulting in them moving out to Turkey and buying an apartment and a restaurant with their life savings are basically putting their lives in the lap of the gods. You will hear people saying that a relationship is all about give and take, well unfortunately if you decide to get involved with a love rat and move to Turkey I'm afraid it will be mostly take. Many ladies however do things blindly without doing any background checking on the Turkish culture. For an older lady to lose her life savings is not only devastating for her but also for her family too.

Sometimes it becomes really precarious because maybe he isn't a love rat and, if that is the case, it's then you move to the top of the ladder and become one of the elite five percenters who have actually made it to some form of meaningful relationship with a Turk, though it will probably be your own money that's financed it. But what are the warning signs that he could be a love rat? My answer to that is you have probably seen those warning signs many times but chose to ignore them. Once he has secured whatever he was after, for sure, a love rat will quickly lose all respect for you and you will quickly lose any control over your restaurant and finances. You could find yourself wanting to just go home but possibly having no finances to get back and possibly even nowhere to live… maybe he isn't a love rat? So when I say by moving out to Turkey you are putting your lives in the lap of the gods you literally are. Now you're in the five club you've either got a keeper or a love rat, can you be sure? Unfortunately, a small percentage turn out to be love rats and leave their victims devastated and with little else to do but accept the situation.

And then we have the ladies I most admire, the five percenters, the ladies who have been with their Turkish partners for a few years they have been through hell and high water, from the bottom of the ladder they have climbed shedding blood sweat and tears along the way. These ladies have been through all the culturist issues that I had to go through in those early years, they came close to breaking me and it's even tougher for women. These ladies are now married and part of a Turkish family. Some have children, some have converted to Islam some haven't, but they have accepted the Turkish way of life as difficult as it is, embraced it and my heart goes out to you all. I have a couple of friends who I thought it wouldn't turn out for, but it did and nothing gave me more pleasure than to have been proved wrong…these ladies are legends! The only major problem I have with five percenters is that they give the twenty five percenters just embarking on their journey hope and they will cling on to that hope that maybe one day, despite what everyone tells them, their general thinking is "I know a lady who is a five percenter and one day I will be one of them!"

Basically you can search Google until your blue in the face looking for the warning signs of a love rat and I could give you lots but the chances are you have seen them all and chose to ignore them which I totally understand as you have probably been programmed to believe everything he tells you is true and anything else is just jealous people lying. So here is my best game changer…

If your Turkish lover asks you to lend or give him money (usually one and the same) then forget what you thought you had, put your big pants on and run as fast as your legs will carry you! It may start at a few hundred pounds for various reasons (the family member in hospital is a common one but I've heard them all over the years) that is just the beginning of the slippery slope, you will soon find yourself and possibly your family in a whole load of financial misery. No decent man anywhere in the world

should ever ask his "girlfriend" for money but for Muslims it's Haraam (prohibited in the Koran).
It is written in the Koran as the twenty third immortal sin…
"Stealing through theft (through theft or robbery) is impermissible (Haraam) according to the Quaran Sunnah and consensus of scholars (lijmaa). The Shari'ah penal code considers both theft and robbery as serious crimes against the Muslim faith."

To sum up how you perceived this chapter depends on how far you are on in your Turkish romance, for someone in the early stages they will be hate my writings for someone who has loved and lost then I hope you find some comfort in knowing that you're not alone.

I heard recently on some Turkish love rats page someone suggesting that as a man I can't comment on this subject and that only a woman can understand these things. I don't profess to know a woman's heartache in a break up but from a man who ate, lived and worked alongside Turks sixteen hours a day, seven days a week for six months solid I can only tell you what I've experienced from a resort workers in the hope that you may avoid such heartache.

Phewww, glad that chapters over, now let's get back to my comfort zone, my story!

9

Turkey the Last Hurrah, Nothing Left but Skin and Bones

Eighteenth of June two thousand and four, Tilburg, The Netherlands and what is supposed to be a person's happiest day of their life. My wedding day and I'm in the car with my best mate Karl who had come over from Hull to be my best man.

"I can't do this mate," I said bringing the car to an abrupt stop.

"You're just a selfish bastard! I've come all the way from Hull, it's the first time I've ever been a best man and you're not going to go through with it? Took me ages to write this speech," he said whilst reaching into his pocket to reveal about ten pages! "What about all your family who have travelled over for your big day?" He did have a point, but I seriously considered turning the car around, driving to Eindhoven airport and getting the fuck out of there!

Everything was fine when I arrived in The Netherlands two years previously, however that was only short lived and after a six month honeymoon period we both started to reveal our true selves. Andrea was one of my customers in Omar Sharif's for a couple of years and I think she expected me to be the same crazy guy who used to be dancing on the bar every night and I expected her to be the same fun-loving holidaymaker who used to come and spend her holiday in Omar Sharif's. The year before was the first time I had ever properly gone to Marmaris on holiday and I should have realised then that it wasn't going to work as she didn't want to go Marmaris and didn't like me spending time with my friends there. I resented her for that. Most women would love the fact that I knew a lot of Turkish friends there and they would see a different side to Turkey, but she hated the fact so much and didn't hide her feelings which, at times, was embarrassing. I totally get the fact that she wanted me to herself but unfortunately when she signed up for me she signed up for Marmaris. Although she agreed initially, it was evident that she wanted me to try and forget about Turkey. That was never going to happen, especially with my best mate Denny still there. The holiday turned into a nightmare as it was the night I had the fight with the staff in Armutalan which I think would put anybody off me. But she soon realised just how many friends I had in Marmaris as they all rallied around me.

After the holiday, I think at the back of her mind she was frightened I would return. I totally understood this which is why I didn't return for a while and tried to force myself to settle down. Hence the Day had arrived, the day I had been dreading… my wedding day!

Apart from our relationship, I loved The Netherlands. I had left the metal factory and gone to work for an Irish company that had opened a huge warehouse in Tilburg. I became their inventory manager. We had, six months earlier, bought our own house. Life was good and I had

more money than I'd had for years. I had also made many new British friends at my new place of work, friends who supported me for the next few years of misery. I thank those friends today from the bottom of my heart.
So here I was saying my wedding vows in front of my family. My children and other members of my family had all come across from Hull for the big day. It was a lavish affair with double-decker buses and everything. However, as the wedding video showed, even cutting the cake we were like cat and dog.

Time went on and things only got worse between Andrea and I, she was a beautiful woman but underneath she was a hard woman to live with and resented my British friends for reasons only known to herself. She also had a very sharp tongue in drink. I'm not putting all the blame for our poor relationship on her but she never got my mentality and I struggled to understand hers. I always dreamt that Dutch women were fun-loving, great in bed and free thinking. She was none of the above. Apparently most Dutch woman like to be the boss and this was something that my old fashioned ways would never allow. If she thought I was coming home from a twelve hour shift and cleaning the windows then she seriously needed to think again! Dutch men apparently, more fool them. I am not, nor have I ever been, a chauvinist. I have no issue with doing things around the house. However she was relentless in her requests for me to do things. I had a call from her while I was at work one day, my Mam and Stan had come from Hull to stay with us for the week, she called me up raging because my dad had a shower and left some hair in the sinkhole and she wanted them to leave our house immediately and get a Hotel, as If I was going to tell them to do that!

I loved going to work at Walsh Western, we had a great bunch of British lads there and it was the only chance I got to have a laugh and that we did. It kept me sane although some of the lads' antics were far from sane. I could write a whole book just about my times there.
I still had calls from Denny and friends in Marmaris asking me when I was going back over but although I got itchy feet before the season started I was relatively settled. I still spoke with Sevil once in a while although I daren't tell her I was married.

The final straw eventually came and the event that put a nail in the coffin was when Andrea wanted to start a family. No matter how much we tried it just was never going to happen and I suppose that was a godsend. We both had tests and although Andrea blamed me for her monthly disappointment, the truth was my test showed I had swimmers that could have swum the channel and it quickly became apparent the problem lay firmly with Andrea. That destroyed her, as it would with any woman. Although I expressed my disappointment with her not being able to conceive, deep down I felt it was a blessing in disguise otherwise this book would have stopped here!

I'm not going to bore you with the following few years but let's just say for the first time in my life I had everything a normal person would want, a great job, my own house and plenty of money. However I was no normal person and despite having it all, Andrea was making my life intolerable. Yes we did go to Turkey but she would never go to Marmaris, it was always Alayna or Antalya, miles away from my friends, miles away from my second home. Just being in Turkey though was bringing back the fire in my stomach and I found myself yearning to go back for one last season. Back in Tilburg I found myself going out with the lads more frequently and around that time although I was a social drinker I got into another habit that I used to try and soften the blow of my mundane home life… smoking cannabis. With a coffee shop (where weed was plentiful) a hundred yards from my house I quickly developed a habit. On top of that I would always have a few cheeky lines of cocaine when I was out with the lads and my poor mental health was rearing its head. I can't lay the blame solely with Andrea. I like to think I'm a pretty easy-going fella to live with but I was rapidly losing hope of a future in The Netherlands with her. I suppose around that time I wasn't thinking straight and I knew I had to get out of there. I had one problem that was stopping me, I needed a divorce. I needed some money back from our house and most of all I needed a break from her. What I found strange is, although I knew deep down she loved me, she had a strange way of showing it. I've always appeared, on the outside, to be a confident bloke but this was only a smokescreen to hide my depression and at the time I felt I was fighting a lost cause.

The days of mobile phones was upon us and I kept regular contact with the lads in Marmaris, especially of course Denny who, come March/April time, would try and convince me to work the summer season. I had resisted for the past few years but the more difficult my life got back in the Netherlands the more the idea of returning was a seed that, with a little bit of water from Denny and my ex boss, would grow and grow… it did. My cannabis habit was increasing, my friends were all either settling down or moving on abroad, my depression was worsening, I was losing weight and my marriage to Andrea was almost broke although strangely she couldn't see it. I needed out. I didn't want to go back to the UK. I needed to go back to a place where I felt valued, a place that I loved dearly and it loved me back in return, my happy place where every happy memory I ever had was made. I wanted Turkey and it appeared she wanted me. I had this illusion that a season would change me back to the person I was, how wrong I was!

The problem I had was how the hell could I spin this to Andrea. I suppose it was a no brainer really because I was going anyway. But selfishly I knew I needed a divorce and I needed my investment in the house so it wasn't a case of packing my things and off I went. I had to be upfront and honest and as much as I wanted to go it wasn't going to be easy explaining my reasoning to Andrea.

Many questions entered my head that winter of 2007, at forty two was I too old for working the resorts, what job would I be going back to and where would I live? That February of 2008, I received a phone call from both Denny and his boss, Ilhan. It was then that the seed Denny had planted in my head had grown and flowered. Ilhan had a new hotel on the beach and below it was Bacchus show bar. İlhan had big plans that summer to transform Bacchus into a drag show act to rival the Talk of the Town and he wanted me to run the entertainment side of it, nothing else. My salary was a great one and I would be given my apartment back in Armutalan at Club Sera. My work visa would be assured and the selling point was that I would be living next door to Denny! So the only remaining question I had was "did I still have it in me?" I needed to know once and for all because if I didn't that would close the door firmly to any future of working the resorts… I wouldn't know that unless I tried.

Telling Andrea was never going to be easy but I needed to leave the option of returning to The Netherlands open so I had to play this very carefully. Although far from happy I think she knew this day would come as not a day went by without us arguing. Basically we weren't meant to be but now was not the time to tell her. After a week or so pondering on it she reluctantly agreed to me going to work in Marmaris. I said I would send money to her every month and that she could always come and stay with me when she wanted and it would be one season and one season only.

My boss at the warehouse in Tilburg, who was also a good friend at the time, also couldn't get his head around it but assured me that should it all go tits up my job would always be open. As crazy as it seems boarding the plane at Eindhoven airport that March I knew it wasn't right, I didn't feel it, maybe Marmaris had changed, maybe all my friends had moved on, maybe I couldn't hack it anymore and maybe, just maybe I would never return to The Netherlands. In hindsight my fears were all justified, the last few years in The Netherlands had taken their toll, I was broken, would Marmaris change all that?… It wouldn't however much I tried.

Having been picked up from Dalaman and driving back through Armutalan I just couldn't believe how much everything had changed. Hotels and apartments were shooting up everywhere! Mine and Denny's drinking hole had been knocked down and turned into some cheesy dance bar! But one thing that hadn't changed though was club Sera.

Obviously the first person I saw was Denny trying to carry a wardrobe by himself up a flight of stairs, so having give him a hand we put it down and had a hug. My apartment was exactly the same as I'd left it a few years ago and it felt like I had never left. Denny had transformed his apartment into a really nice cosy flat with the help of a lady he was now living with who we shall call Brenda. She was a lady from his neck of the woods who had come on holiday, fallen in love with Denny and moved out to live with him. I liked Brenda, she was a large no nonsense woman who looked after Denny and believe me, it was what he needed. Denny had struggled financially that winter as was usually the case.

Now what would normally happen on my arrival for the summer season, Denny and I would get scrubbed up go on a bender and cause mayhem, these benders could go on for days. But this night was different, very different. It started in the usual way, we went to the market. I knew Denny straight away had been avoiding the local market as when we walked in the shopkeeper held up a list of Denny's winter bill which consisted of mainly cigarettes. Fortunately Denny smoked a brand called Maltepe, the cheapest most disgusting cigarette on the market. They were like the Greek cigarettes you bought in the eighties, foul! Even when I was at my most desperate for a fag I would rather refrain than smoke them, but these were Denny's choice of smoke and at twenty pence a packet I was sort of relieved that his bill was only thirty quid. So having bought a few bags of groceries for him and Brenda and settling his bill I also bought us a dozen bottles of Efes and the obligatory bottle of Raki. We headed back to his apartment. Amongst the groceries was this huge fresh chicken and with Denny having one of those old-fashioned stoves powered by fire we proceeded to roast the chicken and crack on with the booze. The smell of that chicken roasting lives with me to this day. As we settled down to chicken salad and a copy of the latest film King Kong. I couldn't help but notice a change in Denny.

Normally he would have sunk three beers and a couple of Raki's before I had finished my first but it was Brenda and I who proceeded to get drunk and Denny was drinking just to be sociable. That night was surreal and as I staggered into my apartment and laid on my bed my thoughts were of how happy I was that Denny was finally settled down. With Denny working at Sera Beach that season and me working a half a mile's walk down the beach at Bacchus, I would need a new drinking companion and the very next day I would meet him.

A knock at my door in the morning and there was Brenda with my morning cuppa, I could get used to this I thought as I sat on my balcony and it was then, with a knock on my door, that my new drinking buddy appeared and introduced himself as Jimmy, Denny's substitute. Jimmy didn't look like a Turk, didn't act like a Turk and engaged in all things non Islamic. I had come across his type before on only a couple of occasion but his English was great and it appeared we had a lot in common, mainly our love of music and especially Pink Floyd. Jimmy was the manager of the Chinese restaurant next to Bacchus and as quick as he was coming into my story, a few months down the line he would tragically leave it and as you will read later I once again escaped death by the skin of my teeth.

Denny and I decided to walk the thirty minute hike down to Bacchus as Denny was doing some work down there. When we arrived, I was greeted by my boss Ilhan, who apart from owning Bacchus also owned the forty room hotel above it. I had been to Bacchus a few times in the past but the restaurant was having a major overhaul. The swimming pool had been filled in to make way for the stage and it seems they were serious about making this a major contender to Talk of the Town in what looked like a very costly refurbishment.

Ilhan explained my job role that summer which mainly involved me organising the evening's entertainment. I would be doing two tribute acts, Frank Sinatra and Neil Diamond, something I'd done in clubs and pubs many times over the years.

I have never been able to cope with Marmaris in winter, the ex-pats love it but for me it bores me to tears. I think the longest I have done is two months back in nineteen ninety-eight. I simply cannot handle a quiet Marmaris and although it's a lot busier these days back in the day it was as dead as a doornail, and you were lucky to see a handful of cars all day. So, after having had my duties explained it was a case of waiting for the season to start.

I would have to wait six more weeks without my sidekick who would be working at Sera Beach again that season, so I turned to Jimmy who, apart from me, was the only staff member there that March. Everywhere I went I had heard that Jimmy was crazy… even Denny himself said so! But I liked crazy and if Jimmy was to step into Denny's shoes then I was hoping he lived up to his reputation.

With Denny now settled he didn't come out on a night so it was me and Jimmy who would sit there on the beach every night with a fire and a bottle of JD, listening to music and talking till the early hours. We would occasionally head up to what is now the viewing point just outside of Marmaris, everyone's favourite view high up looking over İçmeler. We would take a BBQ up there and those nights were special. One thing Jimmy had that Denny didn't was transport and that was in the form of a big Harley Davison type chopper. This was handy as with him being my neighbour I had no need to catch a dolmuş to and from work.

Going into April and finally Marmaris was starting to wake up and staff were slowly arriving. It was always a good time for me as friends old and new started to arrive. With some bars starting to open I would go for drinks with old friends, one in particular was Mehmet from River Jewellery who already was discussing business and my commission that season. With his shop being just behind Bacchus it looked like it could be a bumper season for my gold commission.

Another face had appeared that March, DJ Nimo. I was expecting him as I asked for him specifically because the lad was a genius with sound systems and lighting. In my opinion he still is one of the best DJ's I've worked with. I had worked with him previously at Sera Beach and we seemed to click, it was relief to see him arrive.

The worst time for any resort worker was the week before opening and the month of May, the stress can, at times, be unbearable as every boss in resort wished they had not left things until the last minute and struggled to put the finishing touches to their bars/restaurants. With this came stress and lots of it! My boss Ilhan was a total stress head anyway but the tens of thousands of pounds he had invested in Bacchus made it even worse. You know heart attacks in Turkey are common and most of them are brought on by stress and financial worries. İndeed Ilhan was like a cat on a hot tin roof. Having worked for him previously I already knew him well but this season he was at his most stressed and had to go to the hospital a couple of times before the season had even started.

Myself with the girls from Bacchus

Myself and our waiters at Bacchus 2008

These posters where all over the place

With the girls in our team

Another full house at Bacchu

My mate Jimmy, shine on you crazy diamond

I had plenty of things to think about during those long pre season days/nights but again I was drinking too much. My calls to Andrea became less frequent as I was half cut most of the time and also because myself and Nimo were busy preparing everything needed to ensure we had the best sound and light show in Marmaris. As far as preparation was concerned we were, surprisingly, on track. Nimo was a perfectionist. His new DJ box had every state-of-the-art gadgets imaginable and boy did he know how to use them. I did see Denny in the mornings as he popped in with a cuppa and we would sit on my balcony and talk about the past seasons. But Denny had changed and to be honest he wasn't getting any younger so he needed to. Although what I will say is that Denny never stopped working and for his age was as strong as an Ox. Sometimes people underestimated him, those that knew him kept out of his way when he was about to blow a fuse, those that didn't felt the wrath of him. Staff simply play acting with him when he was in a mood would feel his full force and believe me when he lost it, he lost it big time. As well as seeing Denny every morning I also had Brenda doing my cleaning and Ironing for a small cost. That was until she got a job at Bacchus as a barmaid and I had to fend for myself!

Slowly but surely our staff arrived, I knew a couple of them and I was introduced to the rest of the team and on paper it looked a strong one. The drag team also arrived along with all their stage clothes which must have cost them a small fortune in excess luggage! They were three lads who had previously done seasons in Blackpool and were new to working in Turkey. I just knew their excitement would quickly turn to disappointment as they were about to about to embark on the Turkish system of working. Although I didn't get involved, I knew it wouldn't be long before they found out that working Turkish resorts was far from a six month party. They were indeed professional but professionalism is just a small part of enduring a season in Turkey and although I was to work with them every night the relationship would be strictly business as I had my own demons to conquer. So it was, for me, a case of "I'm alright pull the ladder up". This was something only experience had taught me from that very first season back in Omar's. That first week of the season however, I was about to commit the immortal sin and went against everything I had learned.

And so the curtain opened on that first day of the season. May 2000 and the resort owners proudly showed off their refurbished bars and restaurants. All they needed now were customers. It's a really bizarre time those first two weeks of the season. The Turks truly believe that Dalaman will have aeroplanes coming fully packed with customers eager to spend their money. Historically, however, it never works like that. The fact is, the few aeroplanes that actually come early season have very few tourists aboard. The passengers are mainly made up of girlfriends coming to see their boyfriends, reps and resort workers. The few tourists you do get are regulars eager to get a fix after a long six months of rattling for their addiction.

Although I kept my mouth shut, the feedback I was getting from Thomas Cook reps was that they were struggling to sell holidays mainly due to the fact that eighteen months prior in Marmaris there had been a terrorist attack on a dolmuş in which ten British tourists had been injured. This year the PKK were warning tourists not to visit Turkish resorts in the summer. In fact, a bomb went off literally two hundred yards away from Bacchus outside what used to be the original MacDonald's on the main road.

Although I didn't really have to work during the day I'm not one for being sat about doing nothing. I hated the sun and didn't sunbathe so I would go down to Bacchus during the day and try and hassle the few tourists that walked the beach. Denny and I were about half a mile's walk along the beach from each other but I did try and get to see him when I could. On one particular day I thought I'd go and see how he was doing down at Sera Beach. He had had a major input on the refurb there and had turned it into like a Geordie bar right down to the black and white floor tiles. On the walk down there I would stop and talk with friends along the beach and this is when I saw a Turkish bloke completely dressed in orange hassling outside his restaurant. I sat watching him bringing in the very few Dutch tourists with great success and although I should have ignored it I had a light bulb moment so struck up a conversation with him. Mehmet was from a district of The Netherlands called Utrecht, he was born in Turkey but moved over to The Netherlands when he was a child which explained why he spoke fluent Dutch but he also spoke excellent English which told me he had been educated in a Dutch school. Having sat chatting with him for a while I liked Mehmet, I also liked the way he worked and I wanted him to come and work with me at Bacchus.

He was a European Turk and this was his first time working a resort and I felt he could offer us a lot as his bar was full of Dutch people so I innocently put the idea of him coming to work with me to him and he was up for it. Obviously I had to put this to Ilhan which I did that afternoon. He liked my idea although told me it was on my head to which I agreed. The next day Mehmet started at Bacchus and I proudly stood back while he went about hassling and wasn't surprised to see him catching all the Dutch tourists that passed. I spoke pretty good Dutch myself but obviously this kid was the real deal.

Ilhan was extremely happy with the situation those first few days and then it all went Pete Tong. I came into Bacchus one day and saw Mehmet in the restaurant next door drinking coffee something that simply isn't done and when I finally got his attention he came out and I explained to him that he shouldn't do that again. I was just glad Ilhan didn't see him otherwise he would have been sacked immediately. I cannot stipulate enough how Turkish restaurants owners feel about their staff spending time in a rival's bar. It's simply not done! The way they see it is that if you are seen drinking in places other than their own then what does it say about their place. I totally get that and learned that in my early days. Nothing winds a Turkish boss up more. I think the message got through to Mehmet but there was a lot more to come as I would often get involved in his arguments with our staff and some got pretty nasty. Mehmet would not acknowledge the Kurds working in Bacchus, he was above them and had the mindset from years gone by when the Kurds didn't have the power they have now. He spoke to them like dogs, expected them to run about after him and in his eyes he was never going to take instructions from any Kurd. I knew the time would come when I got pulled into the office by Ilhan for this and that day inevitably came.

Even though I wasn't brought there to hassle, I had nothing better to do and the truth is I was good at it and I enjoyed it. However a large group of Brits passed and I couldn't get them in and I saw Ilhan standing watching, he shouted over to me. We went into the office and he tore into me, the normally passive Ilhan turned into a raging madman which resulted in us both scuffling in the office and me telling him to shove his fucking job. He also reminded me that I had brought Mehmet to Bacchus and all he had done was cause trouble so either I told Mehmet to pack his stuff and leave or he would! I stormed off and tried to calm myself down going on a pub crawl and getting wrecked before being awoken by Jimmy telling me Ilhan wanted to see me. So off I went on the back of Jimmy's bike and was greeted like a long-lost friend by Ilhan who apologised. We kissed and made up but over the next couple of days I realised I had made a rod for my own back having to listen to Mehmet telling me that Kurds don't belong in his country. I sat down with him many times and as much as this Englishman tried to tell a patriotic Turk that times had changed he couldn't except it. The final straw came one day when I went to Bacchus and Mehmet was sporting a gold bracelet. He explained that his Dutch friends/customers had bought him it. I knew the customers, they were elderly and whether it was the case or not I believe he groomed them for it. So I gave Mehmet a couple of days to pack his bags and find a new job which he did amicably and we said our goodbyes.

Turks brought up in Europe become modernised and ignorant to the changes in Turkey, they try to bring their European mentalities to their own country and it doesn't work. When it comes to how the Turkish resorts work, I should have known better than to bring Mehmet to Bacchus. You will probably recall when we got closed down in Omar Sharif's all because the boss's brother came for a holiday and was left in charge one night. He thought it was normal to speak to the Turkish police like we would talk to them back in the UK.

So we were into the first month and to be fair we were the best of a bad bunch. It appeared our show was dragging in the tourists with the aid of our gigantic show posters which were all over Marmaris. Talk of the Town had the monopoly in Marmaris for years but surely there was room for two drag shows in town?… there was but as tourists were few and far between it was pretty obvious they were going to choose the free option. It got to a point where the bosses from Talk of the Town demanded a meeting between them and our bosses. They weren't happy at the fact that during the show I was mentioning that our show was free and theirs was charging a tenner.

To be fair our show was pretty good being only two months into the season. The guys were professional. I remember listening to Champagne Shirley impersonate Shirley Bassey, it gave me goosebumps!

The drags had endured their first month and I knew the time would come when they got their bar bill. They had told me they were told they would get a discount on the food and drinks but when you're drinking as much as they were it soon added up and when the day came to pay they weren't happy at all. They also came up against the Turkish resort pay system when you have to use the much-needed negotiating skills Yunus taught me all those years ago. I think they threatened to go home a few times before the boss finally gave in and paid them.

I smiled to myself backstage when I saw the copious amount of Vodka behind the curtain and I would often have a few with them before we went on. I also had the pleasure of watching four men dressed in girdles and tights getting ready and the endless piss taking I had to take from them. When I announced them onstage we were all pissed but they put on a great show which gave us a full house every night. I was getting pretty famous and I was often asked for my autograph (fame at last).

As for me, I was drinking far too much and falling into my old habits. I spent a lot of the day hassling at Bacchus in between working on the nights programme and having to deal with complaints from our hotel guests, but I was coping. I often saw Denny in the morning and we would have a brew and a chat and I could tell that Denny had started doing his Tina Turner as we were once again getting some funny looks on the dolmus because of

Denny's bright red painted false nails glued on with superglue.

Sometimes we would walk down to the front and walking with Denny was always entertaining. He knew everyone including the local constabulary who would sound their horn to him or stop the car to speak with him. Unfortunately with Denny's limited Turkish vocabulary his greeting would always be, "Ne haber lan pezevenk," and they would be in hysterics. Denny was asking them in a really bad slang "how are you pimps?". Now to say that to any Turk you are going to get yourself into serious trouble but to say it to the ruthless Turkish police well, only he could get away with that! Denny was a legend in Marmaris and only he could get away with it. Pezevenk is a really offensive word in Turkish which I never got because it means pimp. To call someone that in the UK wouldn't be a big issue but never even mutter this word whilst in Turkey. When a lady police officer pulled up to Denny one morning he greeted her in the same way and when I explained that as a woman she couldn't really be a pimp his answer was, "Ah well she's a lady pezevenk then." In those days Denny was an iconic figure to everyone in Marmaris, from street cleaners to the mayor. He was a celebrity and part of Marmaris's furniture. Although they had locked him up a few times for having no visa I think they all gave up in the end. I said to Denny once, "Why don't you just come over to Rhodes with me for your visa?" To which he replied, "To be honest Bonny lad I don't mind Marmaris jail it gives me a break and I can get some kip without being disturbed all the time." Fair point, but that was Denny all over.

It was going into mid June when I was called into the office where Ilhan explained to me that the show was doing well but his brother who managed Sera Beach (Denny's place) needed me to go there for a couple of weeks. I reluctantly agreed but actually fancied a change. It was clear that first night Denny didn't want me there as he had claimed it as his Geordie Bar. I talked him around though and said I wasn't there to interfere in the restaurant side as it was obvious that Denny was getting the tourists in. The trouble was they would eat and then go elsewhere so our mission was to keep them in there. Indeed over the next few weeks we had it bouncing and had put back the cheese Sera Beach was renowned for, the Cheesy Music, Dancing Waiters, Karaoke and Play Your Cards Right.

It was whilst having that stint at Sera Beach I noticed a big change in Denny, he wasn't drinking so much and would disappear to his room in the afternoon, not to sleep I was to later discover but to read the Koran.

I think Sera Beach sapped me of my energy as when I returned back to Bacchus I was running on empty and taking in way too much sun as well as not eating much at all. But I got through June and then July hit us with a heatwave that led me to retire from hassling in the daytime sun and spending more time drinking with Jimmy. The Chinese restaurant that Jimmy was the manager of was next door to Bacchus and sometimes I helped out in there and it amused me how fickle British tourists were, the two restaurants were both owned by my boss and unknown to the customers shared the same kitchen and chef and how I kept my mouth shut when customers would tell me their meal had been superb and that they had exactly the same food the previous night in Bacchus and it was garbage even though it was cooked by the same chef in exactly the same way. Now Bacchus was always busy so the staff had very little time for banter with the customers whereas the Chinese restaurant was fairly small so they waiters had plenty of time to spend time with the customer and make them feel special and that is so, so important, making customers feel special it can turn a bang average meal into a fantastic one!

I had heard rumours about Brenda and a young barman from Bacchus but put it down to idle gossip. However one morning, after jumping off the dolmus, I was walking toward the beach and I saw a figure on the other side of the road. It was Brenda all dressed up from the night before. I don't know if she saw me but I changed direction and headed up to see Denny at Sera Beach. When I got there, he was in bits. Brenda hadn't returned home and he was frantic. I know I should have told him but I couldn't bring myself to do it. I very rarely saw Denny phased but he was devastated and wasn't ever the same after that, obviously I never talked with Brenda after that, she knew that I knew and I left it at that.

The routine for me back then never changed, I would drink a small bottle of Raki and have my afternoon nap. I would get up shower and like clockwork Jimmy would be knocking on my door at 5.30pm for work. We would smoke fags, listen to music and we would jump on his motor bike and off to work we would go. But one night was going to be the luckiest night of my life and for me it felt like my nine lives were almost up. The knock came at my door and in waltzed Jimmy, his usual self and after a few cigs and a beer we stood up to leave when my mobile rang and it was Ilhan telling me he would be picking me up in five minutes as we needed to go and get some new disco lights from the centre. I said my goodbyes to Jimmy and sure enough Ilhan picked me up and off we went. After getting the lights we returned to a rather subdued Bacchus and everyone was mumbling to each other. Murat, our head waiter, pulled me aside and told me that Jimmy was on his way to work, had an accident with a taxi and had been rushed to hospital with what was described as life threatening injuries. Jimmy lay in a Coma in Mugla hospital for two weeks before they turned the life support machine off. It transpired that Jimmy had for some reason not come to work via our usual route. I got it into my mind that if I had been on the back of the bike that night he wouldn't have changed his route or would he have? Once again I had dodged a bullet in Turkey and it wasn't felt I was ready to go yet. With this in mind I stumbled my way through to mid-August but in truth I was finished, broken and living from day to day hoping for the days to become shorter and the season to end quickly. They never did though, the days got longer and October seemed a million miles away.

Andrea had visited me twice that season and called me to say she would be coming early September. I broke down on the phone with her and I think she was relieved when I told her I had had enough and wanted to come home. She did arrive that September and what greeted her brought her to tears, I had lost a lot of weight, I looked terrible, I was drinking heavily and my depression was as bad as it ever got. I had a conversation with Ilhan and told him I was going to have a week off and then I was going back to the Netherlands which he was far from happy about. I explained that the show had been a great success and that he didn't really need me, he reluctantly agreed.

The holiday gave me chance to say goodbye to my friends and one in particular Denny. I met him in a bar and it was quite clear Denny was struggling. He looked washed out and tired and that night (see photo) I literally begged him to go home for a while to which he agreed and that I would meet him at Dianna travel the following morning and buy him a ticket home. The hands in the air was his promise to me he would be there. Despite waiting an hour for him and trying to contact him, Denny never showed up that morning and the time when that photo was taken was to be the last time I saw him alive.

Going through Dalaman that day I popped to the toilet and looked in the mirror to see what came back at me. I looked like someone who had spent the last five months laid under a sunbed smoking crack! As the plane left the tarmac of Dalaman I was sad but also relieved. A glance across at Andrea showed she was like a cat that got the cream. She came to rescue me and in truth she did, but that flight home was a time to reflect. Although it broke me it was well worth putting myself through that season but it became evident that no forty-year-old could work a full on summer season, unless you're called Denny that is!

Marmaris had spoilt me, it had made me arrogant to everything and everybody as I knew if the shit hit the fan or things weren't going my way I could simply jump on a plane and Turkey always had her arms open for me. I needed that season so much, I needed to close that door but knew I couldn't, while that door was open then I couldn't settle down, I couldn't make promises and at forty three I needed to. I owed it to myself and everyone close to me to close that door. On landing at Eindhoven airport I promised myself I would make a concerted effort, accept my responsibilities and grow the fuck up!

On my return to the Netherlands I called my old boss and true to his word I got my job back, although I would have to start from the bottom again. My boss reassured me though that I would climb the ladder quickly and that I did securing a warehouse manager's role within a month. Things were looking up, once again I became a social drinker and settled down into life.

Andreas family obviously weren't my greatest fans but apart from that and the odd blip we were fine. We were still trying for a baby and Andrea had gone through fertility treatment but every month would end in disappointment and it once again put a strain on our marriage. Then a phone call out the blue was to be the final straw. It was what every Dad wanted to hear and should have made me the happiest man on earth but subsequently it was about to make my next few months turn my already fragile mental health into hell on earth.

"Dad I'm pregnant," came the call from my daughter Corina and like every first time Grandad I was ecstatic and literally jumping with joy. Andrea rushed in to ask what was going on and in hindsight I could have put it better but exclaimed I was going to be a grandad. She went crazy, whatever her reason, be it jealousy or that she knew how important my daughter was to me, Andrea was never keen on Corina. We had been to the UK for her wedding a few years prior and my attention was obviously on proudly giving my daughter away on her wedding day. Andrea resented the fact that my daughter was getting my full attention that day.

The guidelines Andrea laid down after she went ballistic that day were something I could never accept, she didn't ever want to hear talk of the pregnancy again and made my only daughter's pregnancy like some sort of dirty little secret. That was something I couldn't cope with and it got to the point where I was walking on egg shells every time I got a call from the UK. It inevitably brought up a conversation about Corona pregnancy and as the weeks rolled on I went into a place in my life that I had never been and I went into total burn out mode. At the time I had some really good mates in The Netherlands who had my back. When I finally left Andrea they had my back and I always had a place to stay. I started drinking too much, putting far too much coke up my nose and constantly had Andrea attempting to make my life an absolute misery.

I was to sink further those next few weeks when I lost my job. Luckily I had friends around me that always had work for me although not all of it was legitimate. One job that springs to mind was for a friend of mine who was renovating a twenty story block of flats. My job for a month was to sit in my car keeping an eye on the twenty Polish lads working on it and if they stopped working I simply got out of my car and screamed at them to get back to work! I got paid a hundred euros a day for that and a case of beer! I also helped my dodgy Dutch mate build a small warehouse in Amsterdam and when the job finished and I asked for my wages he simply said he couldn't pay me but handed over the keys to his stunning BWM 320i.

I had to get out of the Netherlands but knew I had to put all my affairs in order as it was doubtful I would ever return. The priorities were to get a divorce and to get some of the money back I had invested in the house. I eventually got the divorce however I was going to have to wait two months before I received a settlement payment on the house. So it was a case of having to wait it out and my mental health was quickly deteriorating. If I thought I had a few scary moments in Turkey, those last couple of months in The Netherlands proved to be a battle between myself and those demons.

They say that some people can take their own life in the spur of the moment but I don't buy that. It takes careful planning and anyone who has ever seriously considered ending their life gets to the point when they plan it like a military operation… and that was me. I knew where I was going to do it and how. I would take my car to Willamina Park in Tilburg, attach a hose pipe to my exhaust, drink a bottle of vodka and turn the engine on. I had gone through this scenario a hundred times in my head right down to where I would buy the hosepipe and masking tape. What stopped me though was the thought of never seeing my grandchild and the friends I had around me at the time namely Doug Marshall, Dennis Ward, Alex Murrey and a Dutch friend of mine Paul Van Halteren and his parents who gave me a safe haven to shelter from the storm. That storm was coming thick and fast as Andrea made it as difficult as possible for me to leave.

After eight years of hard work Andrea together with her solicitors offered me a measly payment of five thousand euros which was then three thousand five hundred pounds and although my own solicitor advised to wait it out for a better offer I simply couldn't hang on any longer. Those final three months I turned to my old friend drink to self-medicate and with me no longer capable of work, the days were getting longer and I was on a knife edge.

Getting on that ferry from Rotterdam to Hull was a huge relief, I could breathe. I left with no mention to anyone back home and I soon found myself knocking on Mam's door at 10am that morning. She opened the door to someone she barely recognised, someone who barely recognised himself, but I was home, I was safe.

Hull is my home, my birthplace, but it's not a place I wanted to be. But it offered someone that I urgently needed, my doctor, Dr Leng. He had seen me fall apart fifteen years prior and he was about to come to my help again and quickly referred me to a top psychiatrist. Those sessions were invaluable. Times when things got too much would see me at the reception of his practice literally begging to see him. Cognitive Behaviour Therapy was a relatively new treatment for mental health back in the day and I was one of the first to receive it in Hull. It is designed to change your way of perceiving things. Although a little daunting as every session was recorded via video, it helped and slowly, I was getting back on my feet.

Obviously my first port of call was to visit my newly born grandson Alex, although I was a month late to be in the UK for his birth, it gave me that kick up the backside and I found myself moving to Manchester where I had a relationship with a lovely lady called Sue who lived only a few miles from my daughter. It gave me chance to spend as much time as possible with Alex, babysitting him at every opportunity I got and that did me the world of good.

I still had a foot in the door in Turkey and started a Facebook page called Marmaris Holidays, Hotels and General advice which allowed me to sell property and holidays and give advice to holidaymakers which kept me busy. My knowledge of Marmaris meant I had a lot of contacts and I had made a contract with a flight operator and three hotels in Marmaris. It was a relative success back then when booking flight-only and booking hotels direct was a real money saver. Then came the ash cloud over Iceland and caused mayhem in the travel industry and saw me having to re pay thousands back in deposits.

It seemed bad luck followed me as a few months later Sue's only son Ryan got diagnosed with testicular cancer and it meant regular trips for us all to Christies hospital in Manchester. It was whilst there and seeing a ward full of young men hooked up to their Chemo drips that humbled me. For all the shit I had been through I was blessed that here I was, a bullet dodger whose great escapes were on a par with Houdini. These teenagers struck by cancer at such an early age inspired me. Thankfully after a few hairy moments Ryan got the all clear and asked me to help him form a charity called "Lease of Life". We went on to raise thousands for young people with cancer. It also meant me having to climb Ben Nevis for the cause and in two thousand and twelve along with forty other fund raisers we did it!

I also found employment in the UK for the first time in years, at Tescos of all places, on the Deli counter. My duties involved working on the meat, fish, cheese and the make your own pizza counter. I lasted a couple of years but stuck at it before my Mam took ill and I needed to get back to Hull.

I also received a call from Turkey informing me that Denny had passed away. I knew he had a couple of minor heart attacks since I had left Marmaris but I can just imagine the stubborn old sod disregarding all the advice he had been given from his GP and carried on regardless. Apparently, Denny suffered a massive heart attack that April of two thousand and thirteen and it broke me. As you are probably aware an Islamic funeral usually takes place within twenty-four hours after death. Sadly with work commitments and with Dalaman being closed to external flights, there was just no way I was going to make the funeral. I did see his funeral on Marmaris TV and he received a full Islamic burial. This was a shock to many people as it was only at his autopsy that it was discovered that he had converted to Islam and told no-one. The funeral was attended by many and included the many friends Denny had amassed over the years as well as the mayor of Marmaris who actually spoke highly of Denny. Throughout all my sadness I still had a little chuckle to myself, Denny always swore he would see me out working in Marmaris and he did just that. I could hear him looking down on me and saying, "I told you I would pezevent." Denny did get the wish that he told me years before, he wanted to die in Marmaris and to be buried in Armutalan cemetery where he lies today. But I'm thinking his soul had gone to paradise and he will be up there talking peoples' heads off. For any of you who may be interested, if you type Denny Larkin in YouTube you can watch the ceremony. Ten years on and Denny remains an icon. He was and always will be a legend in Marmaris and I'm hoping that, after reading our adventures together in the early days, you may not have met him but I'm sure you can imagine what a character he was. Still to this day on my holidays to Marmaris, I see him, I hear him and he haunts me with Simply the Best and Hotel California which, by no coincidence, is played in every place I frequent.

So, after a fairly consensual break up with Sue I arrived back in Hull. The problem being I didn't have a job nor a place to call home. Then out of the blue I got a call from an old friend of mine asking me if I would be interested in going back into the licensed trade, something I swore I would never do after leaving the trade in ninety five after ten long years and running many a rough pub around Yorkshire.

Apparently, a couple he knew were looking for someone to manage a pub/restaurant in a picturesque village just outside of Hull. Having met the couple for an interview they offered me the job, the wages were good and more importantly the position would mean me "living in" which at the time was a perfect solution for my dilemmas. Although I was a little apprehensive, I agreed and had a great time running the Fox and Cony in South Cave although I knew It was only going to be a temporary fill in.

I started volunteering at a hostel for young people and I took to it like a fish to water so when the opportunity came to go full time in social care working with challenging youngsters I jumped at the chance. Eight years later I climbed the ladder and found myself where I am to this day, working with youngsters with many kinds of issues. The job is both demanding, challenging and stressful but I love my job. It humbles me and despite the bad days having the chance to change the lives of "my kids" makes it all worthwhile. I say my kids because that's what they are and having supported hundreds of kids over the years, nothing gives me more pleasure than seeing them change their lives around and knowing I had a part to play in that.

As for relationships I had a couple while back in Hull but nothing that was meaningful and then I was hit with another bombshell. I had a call from Stan my stepdad one Thursday night telling me my mum had fallen outside the house and was in hospital and having rushed their found her in good spirits, it was feared she had broken her hip but she was a hard woman my Mam, a real fighter who I often was grateful to have in my corner when the shit hit the fan. Three days later she passed away after complications with her operation. I had sat by her side for those four days whilst she was in hospital and saw her deteriorate. Having gone home one night I was sat having a glass of wine and something told me I had to go back to hospital. Having had a drink I wasn't going to drive but to the bewilderment of my friends who I was with at the time, I simply announced I had to go.

On arrival at the hospital I found my mum lying in her hospital bed with Stan sat asleep in the chair next to her. My Mam was barely conscious and as I held her hand I saw a trickle of blood run from her nose and I knew it was time. My Mam always blamed herself for me never being able to settle. She had walked out of our family home when I was nine and she blamed all my failures on herself. Those final few moments gave me the chance to explain to her that her leaving both my dad, myself and my sister had nothing to do with it. She left for her own reasons but never ever stopped loving us, although I hated her at the time for this and never wanted to see her again. However in time I forgave her and both her and my step dad Stan gave me the best upbringing any young lad would relish. I held her hand that night as she drifted in and out of consciousness and I poured my heart out to her and with a smile on her face she went to heaven. My Mam was always my biggest critic and I would often be on the end of her sharp tongue but anyone else who dared to criticise me would feel her full wrath. She was everything to me, my rock, my diamond and losing her devastated me. To this day I feel her, see her and ask for her guidance.

A couple of months after losing my Mam I got a friend request from a girl I knew from when I was a teenager growing up in Hedon, a village just outside of Hull. At the time I was on holiday in Sidari, Greece and, to be honest, I didn't want a relationship but we chatted for a while and agreed to meet up on my return. We did just that and we laughed when she explained as a nine-year-old how she would sit just staring at me playing football with my mates. I was her first childhood crush and I was about to become her lifetime partner. I honestly believe she was sent to me from my Mam and here we are eight years on. Finally I'm settled with someone who never judged me and someone who I know I will be with until my final breath. As the Stone Roses sang "Until Sally I was never happy", and there has never been a truer word spoken.

As for Turkey, of course I missed Marmaris, it was a huge part of my life. Although I still got itchy feet when the season opened every year that door was closed years ago. I would however "try" and go back as a holidaymaker but deep down I knew I could never go back to Turkey simply as a holidaymaker.

10

A Holidaymaker in Disguise

"I'm going to be a proper holidaymaker this summer" is something I've promised myself and anyone who would listen since I first went back to Turkey post two thousand and eight.

It would be two thousand and fourteen when I finally returned to Marmaris. I had been to Alanya a couple of times and Side, but it didn't really matter, as I've said before the Turkish resort system doesn't only apply to Marmaris it's the same everywhere, exactly the same.

My promise to myself lasted all of an hour wherever I went on holiday I quickly turned to Turkish mode and as much as I tried, I couldn't ever be a holidaymaker. I did try even if it was for only an hour after landing.

Post leaving Marmaris as a resort worker in 2008 I had holidayed in Turkey a few times but it was too soon to return there so I settled for the eastern holiday resorts, Alanya, Antalya and Side but even somewhere where I wasn't recognised. I spent many a late-night eating with new Turkish friends. It's difficult to sit in a restaurant listening to the banter without revealing my true identity although I did find it quite amusing listening to what their opinions of me were and although it was mostly good I once lost it when a group of us went to a restaurant in

Side. We had planned a late one so wanting something light to eat most of us opted for pasta dishes and I knew when ordering what the staff thought. For some reason it gets under a restaurant staff's skin when a full table order pasta. Basically they have this misconception that if people eat pasta or pizza on a night then they are skint and the response we got when ordering was something I expected however what wasn't expected is when I heard the waiter say to the staff, "They are all Gypsies." I went ballistic in Turkish slang needless to say they wasn't expecting that and spent the rest of the night apologising and plying me with free Raki.

I had of course holidayed in different countries Morocco which I hated, Spain which I found really boring, now I can't stand sunbathing, sightseeing and touristy things so the highlight of my holiday in Spain was when I decided I would jump on the first bus to anywhere and this particular bus full of dressed up Spaniards was heading up to the mountains and everyone on board were singing and clapping to which I joined in and after talking to my fellow passengers in pigeon English it seemed I was on a wedding party bus. After we reached our destination I was invited to join them and what a day that turned out to be, free Sangria and Paella were flowing and after treating the wedding party to a few Sinatra love songs for the bride and groom I found myself doing the Flamenco like a pro, I can't remember getting back but I was treated like a long lost friend. Corfu was okay, Greece is a very similar country to Turkey, the food, the landscape, and the weather however it seems the Greeks had got fed up with us Brits over the years. My first holiday as a teenager was in Corfu and I have been many times since, I did a season as a DJ in Ipsos in the late eighties, but it had changed, the Greeks, as lovely as they are, to compare it to Turkey would be a huge mistake, they just don't have the enthusiasm the Turks have for us and the service leaves a lot to be desired but you could say that about every European destination, Turkey is a cut above anywhere when it comes to service and friendliness, in my opinion the best in Europe without a doubt.

After a few years in the wilderness, I was to finally return to Marmaris in May 2014, I remember going on my first proper holiday back there for all the wrong reasons, the first being I spent most of our stay at Alpina apartments arguing with the girl I went there with, the second my beloved Hull City got beat in the FA cup final versus Arsenal after going two up!

With only a week's holiday and between arguing and sunbathing I didn't really have a chance to catch up with old friends, we stayed at Club Alpina in Amutulan and it was a lovely surprise to find that my mentor from the early days Hasan was the hotels photographer. It was lovely to see him again after twenty years and we sat and talked for hours about the old days at Omar Shariff's, I couldn't leave that holiday without seeing my old friend Mikail, the man I owed my life to on a couple of occasions and had my back in the early days, Mikail was now working at Valentinos Jewellers and my holiday wouldn't be complete until I had a walk along the beach front and saw a few old faces, after nearly twenty years their wasn't many although I was still stopped in my tracks asking me if I wanted to work again, one of them being Octay who was now running the Kent bar next to Bacchus and although we didn't always see eye to eye, it was water under the bridge now and we reminisced about the everything from my days in jail to the memories of Denny and in tribute to Denny they had a photo of him hung up proudly in the bar.

Everything was going swimmingly back in the UK now, I was climbing the ladder in my career and I had held my job down for a few years and I was finally growing up and settling down, my Mam's passing in twenty fifteen was a huge set back and broke me but she died proud of what I had finally become and she still talks to me to this very day, mostly to give me a bollocking but a short time after her passing she sent me a gift, a gift that would finally see me settle down to where I am today.

July 2016 and I received a message on Facebook "Is this you Slaz?" now even today when someone calls me Slaz I know it's someone from my distant past as it was my nickname from school so digging further it was a lady from Hedon a town just outside Hull where I grew up. The story goes that she was four years my junior and she used to spend days at her back gate watching me play football with my friends and although only young at the time she went on to tell me I was her first crush, obviously as a teenager myself I wasn't interested in some little girls crush on me but she had dreams that one day I would, and that day came forty years later, I took Sally out a few times before we finally got together that year.

So that was it, at the age of fifty one I had it all. I had been there many times but I knew this was destiny and she was indeed an angel sent to me from my Mam.

Two years in and our relationship and with things going well I obviously spoke often of my past and obviously a lot of it was about Turkey. Sally had never been abroad before so I put the proposition of going to Marmaris with her for a weeks holiday. Knowing that I had a habit of changing into someone else when I went there I purposely chose just seven days in the hope that as had previously happened she would accept that Marmaris wasn't a holiday destination for me it was my home and inevitably as much as I tried I could never go to Marmaris as a holidaymaker, not for the want of trying but I simply couldn't ever go to Marmaris like normal people do. It would mean her meeting my friends for endless nights of doing what Turks do, chatting, eating and drinking copious amounts of Raki. Could she cope with that? Obviously every lady wants to spend their first holiday abroad as a holidaymaker but unfortunately she would see the side of Turkey that not many people do and like myself she would find herself not treated as a tourist but as a local and for some it wasn't easy but for Sally she went with the flow and absolutely loved Marmaris in fact she was addicted and didn't want to go home. It's crazy how I change when I'm in Marmaris, from a mild-mannered Englishman to someone who barters over everything from a watermelon to my bill.

Alanya, a picnic on the river with my old friend Hussain and his wife

Side, with the lads from Beach House

My freind Murat. Twenty five years since I last saw him in Marmaris and he opens a barbers shop in Hull

A special friend from my early days. Emin, remember, the tractor/ taxi driver from chapter 4?

It's difficult for me to holiday in Marmaris, although my Turkish was rusty using Turkish slang was an indicator that I had obviously worked the resorts and the Turkish waiters, most of whom weren't born when I worked there were intrigued as to where I had picked up my resort gutter talk Turkish from. As I said earlier in this book on holiday you are oblivious to what is going on behind the scenes but if you know Turkey and indeed the Turks then you see and hear things that no-one else does and sometimes I wish I didn't.

Arriving back in the UK Sally was already booking our next year's holiday to Marmaris and like many people she spent the next year eagerly awaiting her return there. We have been going every year since, sometimes twice a year and although I sometimes have squabbles with waiters who I think are taking the piss I am changing into a semi holidaymaker, boat trips, shopping, dancing waiter bars and cheesy music, I've done them all something I would never even have considered before.

They say it's a small world but even I could not have anticipated on my journey to work one morning a couple of years ago, driving past a barbers shop that had recently opened in Hull I saw the name Marmaris style barbers and I thought I would investigate and walking in the shop that morning I saw a face I hadn't seen for over twenty five years. Murat, a barber that had a shop literally fifty metres from Omar Shariffs. We spent the rest of the afternoon chatting about the old days and we slipped into Turkish resort slang with fond memories of mutual friends. I regularly go and see Murat these days, not only for a haircut but the banter takes me back to times when things were crazy!

I have many friends in the Turkish community back in Hull. In fact it was when Sally celebrated her fiftieth birthday in my friends restaurant here (Efes) that I came across a waiter there who I knew within minutes had worked the resorts. How did I know? You can tell by both their ability to make a party but also the slang that's only used in resorts. A few weeks later he got into a lot of bother with his boss after allowing me to drink a bottle of Raki on the house and I got that hammered I fell asleep in my Iskender kebab!

I knew most of the Turkish people in Hull in fact both myself and Sally worked really hard to raise money for the recent earthquakes in the East of Turkey and it felt good to be able to do something for what was a terrible disaster.

I still have my Turkish ways, I still can be a big sulker, I hold grudges over silly things that can last forever and I don't take kindly to people who think they can try and belittle me. I make Turkish food regularly and we have spoilt the family on summer BBQ's by making a variety of kebabs, kofte and of course Ayran. My car and house is adourned with Turkish eyes and I often blast my favourite all time singer Ibrahim Tatlises out in my car and sing along like a madman. I eat soup for breakfast always with a squeeze of lemon and a sprinkle of Sumak. I still try and convince myself and Sally that I will be a holidaymaker and I still have many friends old and new in Marmaris. I still keep in touch with old friends and last years holiday saw the worst of me and the best.

We booked for three weeks at T&G apartments last year and the day before we left I said to Sally I didn't feel great as I was getting pains in my stomach however I thought it would pass and we arrived in Marmaris I still wasn't feeling great but put it down to the travelling. After our first night off we went to bed and I woke up at 3am with an insatiable thirst and having drank the full bottle of water next to my bed it wasn't cutting it. I I didn't want to wake Sally up and needed water so I got out of bed and my legs could hardly hold my body up but I managed to walk through reception and across to the shop for more water, I didn't make the shop and collapsed in the road and the next thing I knew I was in the state hospital unaware why I had a drip in my arm and the manager, staff and Sally sat around my bed. The surroundings were like something out of a horror story with bandages and blood strewn across the floor, the fellow in the next bed was snoring and a woman in the far bed was crying hysterically. "Get me the fuck out of here," I said to Sally so at 9am I discharged myself against everyone's wishes, paid the hundred pound bill and without a diagnosis I was wheeled out by the apartments manager who had sat by my side all night. Talking about the manager of T&G apartments Sally never hid the fact that she always thought he was hot and went on to tell me that obviously I had been whisked away in an ambulance without waking her. The manager had to let himself in to our room to tell her and she said she thought all her wishes had come at once as she woke up to find him sat on her bed trying to rouse her! I still didn't feel great but after being filled to the brim with saline I thought I was on the mend, wrong, I went to bed late afternoon and slept through until the morning and drank a couple of gallons of water through the night but in the morning I had horrendous pains in my belly, the doctor was called and I was taken to the privately owned Abu hospital where I had lots of test and scans and I honestly thought after all the near misses I had used up my nine lives in Turkey and I was going to get buried next to Denny in Amutulan. Of all my years working there I had never been to see a doctor never mind been in a hospital and here I was on holiday and saw two in the same number of days!

Here I was laid in my bed going from freezing cold to an inferno every ten minutes and feeling sorry for myself because I hadn't had one visitor and then they all came in together. Apparently in typical Turkish fashion the hospital had mistaken me for the English lad in the next bed and told everyone that called was told that I was sedated and sleeping… After few more hours and I was coming around a bit and apart from shaking profusely in between sweats I managed to get my head together and it's then I stated panicking worrying about Sally being alone in a strange country. My results had come back and I had a liver infection, as much as the Abu is a lovely hospital the English rep for them was really starting to wind me up. She wanted my travel insurance documents which were stored on my phone but obviously with a drip in one hand and my other hand shaking uncontrollably I couldn't open my phone to find them. I explained that I wasn't going anywhere fast and that Sally would sort it out when she came to visit but she just wouldn't take no for an answer and bombarded me with forms to fill in. At this point I'd had enough and told the nurse I was discharging myself and she told me It wasn't wise but me being me told her either she took the drip out or I would be taking it out myself. In the meantime the snotty little hospital rep told me I couldn't leave until the paperwork was filled in for my insurance. Now nobody holds me to ransom and I told her to bring my bill and I would pay it cash and that was that, twelve hundred pounds lighter we got a taxi back to the apartments armed with my daily meds and I went to bed, under strict instructions that I stayed there and I avoided cold drinks, drank luke warm water and could only eat soup, pasta and salad for the ten day duration of my holiday, brilliant. To be fair whilst in hospital friends, staff from restaurants and in particular the amazing staff and reps at the T&G rallied around Sally. My little sister Laura had planned on flying over the next day and if there is one thing I hate whilst I'm not well is fuss. Being the stubborn old git that I am I hate it, I promised everyone I would be on my best behaviour and do as I was told and although It was going to be a boring ten days, sitting in the shade, drinking warm water and eating plain pasta I would do as I was told. One family from our own City of Hull made it a lot easier, The Leck family were seasoned visitors to Marmaris and their antics often brought tears to our eyes but they were a godsend to both Sally and I.

Those ten days on meds were horrendous, If I'm honest I literally scared myself to death and I stuck by the rules but on that tenth day I had my first Efes and it was heaven!

Myself and Octay. Twenty five years of a love/hate relationship. Lovely tribute to Denny above us

With the lads from White Lion

The very last time I saw Denny alive.
Here's the book I promised you Den!

Me with my best Turkish freind Yunus,
rolling back the years

Marmaris bound with the Leck family 2023.
What could possibly go wrong?

Myself and Sal with everybody's favourite view of Marmaris

Coming to the end of the holiday and feeling sorry for myself I received a text out of the blue that was going to make this my best holiday ever.

"Paul I'm coming to see you." Now after years of us trying to arrange to meet that day was here, that day would be tomorrow and after twenty five years of keeping in touch I would tick one off my bucket list as Yunus my first ever true Turkish friend was coming from Izmir to see me!

So like a kid in a sweetshop, we sat there in the apartments bar area waiting for Yunus to arrive, although Sally had never met Yunus she knew him inside out from the stories I had told her and then he appeared and I greeted him with tears of joy like a long lost brother. Obviously now he was a big posh bank manager I asked him which Hotel he was staying and when he told me he hadn't booked into one yet I informed him he was going nowhere and after speaking with the manager, a bed was made up for him in our room and he was going to have to rough it on a fold away bed well, It isn't as if we had both never roughed it before. That night was one of the happiest of my life and it was a relief that his perfect English came flooding back for twenty five years of speaking very little and for Sally's sake we spoke very little Turkish that night only a bit of slang banter.

I smiled to myself that night as we all sat there eating like kings with no expense spared and yet twenty five years prior we were living out of each other's tip box money scraping lira coins together to buy ourselves a pizza from

Megros, As we sat on our balcony talking about the old days I had one last request, Yunus used to get very emotional back in the day when he had too much to drink and getting on for three in the morning with the Raki flowing I said to him I wasn't going to bed until I knew he was drunk, half an hour later he finally had tears in his eyes and I knew it was time to sleep!

The next day and walking Yunus to his car I cried like a baby thinking I would never see him again, I would later that year when he brought his two daughters to see their Uncle Paul and after a great night in Ega Vera we decided to revisit our old stomping ground Greenhouse on Bar Street with his girls. They loved it but I lasted thirty minutes and we scurried home in a taxi. The next day we all jumped in Yunus's car and went off to Akyaka for what turned out to be a lovely day and I actually felt like a real holidaymaker.

"Good friends we have, oh good friends we've lost along the way" wrote the late, great Bob Marley in a song ironically titled "No Woman No Cry" and for all the people I met on my journey in Marmaris I've certainly lost a lot of friends along the way, not passed away but simply lost touch and I often think about them as they played a huge part in my journey. Hamza from Queens Chinese restaurant was one of those, Hamza despite our fall outs was someone who will stay with me forever, he was what I would categorise as a "different kind of Turk" he didn't look like one or behaved like one but he holds a special place in my heart for the support he gave me back in the day. The last time I heard he was working as a petrol pump attendant somewhere in Antalya apparently struggling with an alcohol addiction but I would give my right arm to see him once again. Orhan a Sunquest rep in my early years who I would often be found drinking with in the Bob Marley bar on the marina and of course all the ladies from both Sunquest and Airtours in the late nineties namely Paula and Trish who I would often sit and chat for hours with, Paula in particular who I used to go across to Rhodes with and like myself she struggled with Turkish culture in that very first season. I certainly came across some amazing people, I also crossed paths with a lot of complete idiots. They were forgotten in a second but left a bitter taste in my mouth that lasted a long time most of them being British people who came across to work in Marmaris and made complete fools of themselves.

A true Turkish friend is for life, they are genuine, loyal, caring and have beautiful souls and I would say the vast majority of Turkish people have all these qualities. Yes, they are extremely stubborn, don't like criticism and often sulk for years. They are still for me the most beautiful people on the planet and for sure when your back is against the wall then your Turkish friend will die for you.

On the flip side and fortunately it's very rare a tourist will see it but make an enemy of a Turk then they are ruthless and you're going to get yourself into a shit load of trouble if you make that mistake, I take my hat off to some of the guys I've worked alongside for their patience with holidaymakers because I've seen some really hard Turkish men take abuse off tourists and never batted an eyelid, the same guy I'd seen in winter knock three Turkish guys out with no effort whatsoever…

Remember what I said about a Turkish man's love for money and woman? The British bring both so they can't really afford to get on the wrong side of tourists, especially Brits so they have grown somewhat immune to the Brits on the piss brigade just as I did!

As I laid on my sunbed whilst in Marmaris last year that I decided the day I'd been putting off for years was going to be that day. With no further ado I informed Sally of my intentions.

I had avoided my old neighborhood for years, even during my seasons at Sera Beach and Bacchus I couldn't bring myself to see my old street. Way too many beautiful memories and many difficult ones but as I began my walk down to my old street, I just knew it was something that I had to do.

As I turned down my street it was barely recognisable and after walking the entire length the only things left was Spor Taxi rank on the corner! The rest was history, Omar Sharif was a hardware shop, The roundabout where me and Denny used to share our morning cuppa was gone and as I walked over to Sevil's Hotel I could have cried, the swimming pooled had been filled in, the bars demolished, and it was now offices. As I looked on in sadness, I was ushered out the grounds by some irate Turk not happy I had appeared on his property half crying half taking photographs!

He firmly ejected me from the grounds and locked the gate behind me!

As I returned to the apartment to find Sally laid stuck to her sunbed, she asked me how it went and I told her it went kind of like this…

I turned down my street to find hordes of Tourists heading down to the Friday Market, the street full of vehicles of every description blowing their horns and frantically trying to rid holidaymakers off the road. I passed Faulty Towers where my old friend Ahmet greeted me Kurdish style, across the road and at the Queens Chinese Hamza appeared from nowhere trying to pull me in for a beer and a chicken chow mien. Walking up towards Dennys's restaurant "Paradise" I got chased up the road by the Dog from Simpsons and there he was the legend stood there on a table in his black mini dress, duck slippers and his onions falling out of his bra, my mate, my mukka that crazy fucking Geordie!

Looking across the road to see Carlos sat there naked behind his desk in his dodgy rental place beckoning me in for a Raki! And then down to Omar Shariffs and the music was booming out with the very same music you hear today, the place was packed as it usually was and there stood the DJ responsible for the cheesy tunes banging out from the place, me! Most definitely half cut and in party mode but always in control and always the right arm of my boss Mehmet who never took his eyes off things and entrusted me with everything.

Moving on I passed my good friend Mehmet the market owner next door who I spent many a Raki nights with and then down to Sevil's hotel…

As I approached the Marmaris Sun Hotel I walked in to see the hotel in full flow, the pool full of families, Jacob behind the bar shaking cocktails and "Never ever" playing in the background and then she appeared Sevil, just stood there looking at me and giving me that smile that melted my heart and as I approached her to give her that one last hug I was rudely interrupted from dream by a Turk shouting at me to get off his premises. As I awoke from my dream, I found myself in that very place where my story began. Outside the gates of the Marmaris Sun Hotel, the place where I first stepped foot off my transfer bus and my love affair with Sevil and Turkey began. A story that began for me in ninety eighty seven however this time I wasn't alone because when you opened the very first page of my book, you have lived it with me and I sincerely hope you have enjoyed reading it just as much as I enjoyed living it…

In Memory of Denny Larkin a Marmaris legend.

Simply the Best!

1943-2013

Available worldwide from Amazon

Michael Terence Publishing

www.mtp.agency

mtp.agency

@mtp_agency

Printed in Great Britain
by Amazon

39376537R00155